CW00458314

How To Introvert In An Extrovert World

Michele Connolly

How To Be An Introvert In An Extrovert World

EPUB: 9781925786231
POD: 9781925786248

Earlier versions of the material in this book were previously published in blog
posts on Louder Minds.

Cover design by Red Tally Studios

Publishing services provided by Critical Mass

Contents

How To Use This Book

If you've often felt out of place, overwhelmed by social expectations, or overloaded by the hubbub of life, then this book is for you. It's for the person who's easily overstimulated by light, noise, people. Who enjoys a lot of alone time. Who feels like they wear an extrovert mask to get through large chunks of life.

Much of this book is my own journey from miserable, cantankerous faux extrovert to happy but still delightfully cantankerous introvert. It's how I found self-acceptance and developed much greater acceptance of others, too.

This is not a book you need to read in order. Think of it as your "Introvert Resource Kit" — full of strategies, stories, humor, inspiration, and psychological insights into the introvert life. Start wherever you like, read what draws you in, highlight, re-read, leave lying around for your extroverted loved ones to *accidentally* stumble across.

The goal of this book is to help you understand there's nothing wrong with being an introvert.

To celebrate the pleasures of the introvert life.

To laugh with you about the idiosyncrasies of our introvert tendencies.

To help you accept yourself and others so we all enjoy greater respect and happiness.

Well, that's a lot for one little book — so let's get started!

Part 1: How To Understand What An Introvert Is - And Is Not

Knowing yourself is the beginning of all wisdom.

—*Aristotle*

How To Use The Word "Introvert"

There's a lot of confusion about what exactly an introvert is. Partly this is because there are different ways the word is used.

1. Common Definitions

In common usage, "introverted" is often used as a synonym for "shy". But as any introvert knows, these are not the same things at all. I, for one, am rather an extreme introvert, but I'm not particularly shy. (We talk more about this in *How To Tell The Difference Between Introversion And Shyness*.)

2. Jung

Renowned psychoanalyst Carl Jung wrote of introverts as people who "lose energy" during social interaction, while extroverts "gain energy" from being with others. According to Jung, most people are a mix of the two — anyone who was purely one or the other "would be in the lunatic asylum" (his words, not mine!).

Although there's some evidence for Jung's energy distinction, it's not quite what psychologists mean when they talk about the introversion-extroversion continuum.

3. MBTI

The hugely popular Myers-Briggs Type Indicator extends aspects of Jung's theories and classifies sixteen personality types. Most people enjoy identifying their profile and learning about the implications for their personal and work life. I — an INTJ — sure do.

However, the MBTI does not meet psychologists' requirements for a statistically valid and psycho-metrically sound personality test.

4. Psychology

Psychologists conceive of introverts as being *sensitive to stimulation* — noise, people, lights, everything. Because of this sensitivity, introverts are easily over-stimulated and become uncomfortable with too much input. This explains why many introverts avoid parties and crowds and enjoy simpler, smaller pleasures. Why they cancel plans and crave personal space. Why they register everything that's going on and feel exhausted by it all.

Extroverts, by contrast, tend to need a higher level of stimulation to feel comfortable. For them, plenty of people around and lots going on feels good. Too little stimulation can be unpleasant.

According to psychological research, the tendency toward introversion or extroversion is biologically based and appears to be relatively stable throughout life.

This is not to say that people are born one defined way and stay the same forever. We are all affected by life experiences, different environments, and countless other factors — human psychology is not simple! But there does appear to be a tendency toward introversion or extroversion that's relatively fundamental to our personalities. And understanding this can help us to know ourselves better, to be kinder to ourselves and others, and to enjoy greater happiness.

Because psychologists look to evidence and research to back up their theories, and because my background is psychology, the psychological approach to introversion is the one I take in this book.

How To Understand The Psychology Of Introverts

If you've just picked up this book, you may be wondering what exactly being an introvert means and how to make sense of an introvert personality in an extrovert world. Or you may be wondering what you should have for lunch, which is also a fair and at times troubling question. Either way, I have answers for you (get the burger).

We are all Individuals (I'm not)

Many subjects in psychology focus on what people have in common. Perception, cognition, developmental psychology, neuropsychology, social psychology, even psychopathology — they all look at what's the same about us.

But *personality psychology*, the rebel of the psychology world, is concerned with our individual psychological differences.

The kinds of questions personality psychologists are interested in are:

- How are people different: is there a set of dimensions on which people differ?
- How is an individual unique: can this be scientifically described?

Isn't Personality just for Bad Hair Days?

You could say your personality is made up of those individual differences that are:

- Psychological — as opposed to say, cultural, biological, intellectual, age-related differences
- Enduring — consistent-ish over time and situations, rather than moods or emotions that come and go
- General patterns of thinking, feeling, and behaving — versus specific attitudes or habits.

In the 1930s psychologists tried to figure out how these individual differences might be structured, what the set of dimensions of individual difference might be. (If we were lipsticks, for example, they were looking for aspects like the shade, matte-versus-glossness, degree of pigment, moisturizing quality.)

They began with a dictionary, and searched for all the various adjectives used to describe people.

Yep, really! And it makes sense — can you think of a better starting point?

They then subjected these descriptive words to a cunning statistical method called factor analysis, which allowed them to cull many overlapping descriptors down to underlying, fundamental dimensions.

Over decades it emerged that many studies by different researchers using various data, samples, and assessment methods all yielded the same five dimensions (though different researchers had given them different names). These factors showed considerable reliability and validity (i.e., were psychometrically sound) and also stayed pretty stable throughout adulthood. They were called the "Big Five" because the dimensions were broad and abstract, each subsuming many narrower traits within it.

The idea was, by identifying a person's position on each of these five dimensions, you could get a decent sense of their personality. Not a set-in-stone, perfect-predictor, know-the-person-inside-out sense. Just a rough map of what made this person's psychological terrain different from someone else's. How people differed, and what made them unique.

Today these five factors represent general scientific consensus on personality structure.

Five Things about YOU

So, what are these personality traits?

As you read these, remember they are *dimensions*. You'll fall somewhere along a scale, not 100 percent at one end or the other.

Also remember that there's no value judgment attached. They are essentially the product of *statistical analysis* — nobody is looking down their binomial distribution at you.

1. Extroversion

Although Jung coined the term to describe a tendency to focus on external rather than internal experiences, the modern psychological meaning of extroversion is broader. It encompasses sociability, energy, activity, sensation-seeking, interpersonal dominance, and a tendency to experience positive emotional states. Research suggests the tendency toward introversion or extroversion is biologically based.

- A person high in extroversion could be described as sociable, assertive, enthusiastic, energetic, forceful, talkative.
- A person low in extroversion, i.e., an introverted person, could be described as quiet, reserved, retiring.

2. Agreeableness

Agreeableness reflects cooperativeness, altruism, and compliance. At the other end of the scale is a more calculating, hostile, competitive nature.

3. Conscientiousness

Conscientiousness is largely concerned with goal-directedness and impulse control. At the low end of the scale is impulsiveness and present-orientation.

4. Neuroticism

Neuroticism is a tendency to experience negative emotions including anger, sadness, shame and embarrassment. It does not imply mental disorder. At the other end of the scale is emotional stability, or coping well with stress.

5. Openness to experience

Openness to experience relates to the complexity of a person's mental, experiential, and even aesthetic life. At the other end is conventionality and conservatism.

Discovering your own Personal Personality

There are personality tests that can identify where you fall on each of these dimensions. Such tests will give you pretty much the same answer over time, and whether self-rated or other-rated, they're hard to cheat, they're good at predicting behavior, and they get at something that's real about personality.

But I suspect just by reading the descriptions above you've formed a fair idea of where you fall on each of these dimensions. Or at least you've recognized the dimensions on which you'd score high or low. The personality tests ask you to rate yourself on these kinds of descriptors anyway.

When I read the descriptions I would say I'm:

- Extroversion: very low — like, sub-basement
- Agreeableness: somewhere in the middle
- Conscientiousness: pretty high — borderline pedant
- Neuroticism: toward the high end, which makes me nervous ☺
- Openness to Experience: very high
- Attractiveness: Off the scale high ... Wait, was that not one of them?

Having done the (kind of exhausting) test several times, I know this self-assessment is pretty much spot-on.

What you need to know about the Introvert Personality

As an introvert, or as someone who wants to better understand the introvert(s) in your life, you can now see how the introvert's tendency toward a quiet reserve is part of their psychological make-up. It's one of five fundamental dimensions of individual difference. It's at the core of how we humans differ.

So why do you need to know that? What does it mean?

Well, it *doesn't* mean you have to take a fatalistic view of yourself and feel you're "stuck" being a particular way. Certainly people can and do change over time, and most likely there's a range along each dimension where you can move and still be "you". For example, you can indulge yourself and let your mind run away with you and lean in toward neuroticism, or you can be proactive and work on improving your coping skills and move to the more emotionally stable end of your personal range (something I'm always working on).

It *doesn't* mean you should compare yourself with others and feel inferior. You aren't like the extrovert and you genuinely don't like parties and you truly enjoy quiet evenings in. It's simply a way you're different — it's not a failing!

It also *doesn't* mean you have to listen to the well-meaning advice of others who tell you to "come out of your shell". You can learn what makes you happy, what feels right for you, and know that it's perfectly okay if others don't understand. In fact you shouldn't expect them to understand — their personality is different!

And this is what's so great about personality psychology. By understanding what makes us *different*, we can *appreciate* these differences — both in ourselves and in others.

We can stop judging — both ourselves and others.

We can be kinder and more accepting — toward both ourselves and others.

We can say, Hey, that's just how it is for me, you, him, her, them …

And with this perspective, we can support one another to each be happy in our own, individual, different way.

How To Tell The Difference Between Introversion And Shyness

There are many misconceptions about introverts. A common one is that introversion and shyness are essentially the same thing. In fact, if you google "introverted definition" you'll see "shy" as the first synonym. But psychologically speaking, being an introvert is not the same as being shy.

What is Introversion?

Introverts tend to be easily overstimulated by external environments, people, noise, lights, that kind of thing. They therefore prefer quiet and solitude.

What is Shyness?

By contrast shy people are timid around others and often fear how they'll be judged. Consequently, they tend to be reticent about putting themselves out there where people may form a negative opinion about them.

Can you be both?

There is definite overlap, where people are both introverted and shy, though the extent of the overlap remains unclear.

Venn diagrams to the rescue!

If you love Venn diagrams — and honestly, who doesn't? — then you'll be happy to know that a handy explanatory Venn diagram follows.
As the Venn diagram shows:

- Some people (me included) are **introverted but not shy** — we aren't especially worried about others' negative opinions, but we do like our quiet and solitude.
- Some people are **shy but not introverted** — not particularly vulnerable to external stimulation but concerned about how they are judged and cautious about exposing themselves to judgment.
- Some people are both **shy and introverted**. This is the overlapping part, the intersection.
- People not falling into any of the above categories are **neither introverted nor shy**.

Has this reawakened your long-forgotten love of Venn diagrams? If so, I'll leave you guys alone …

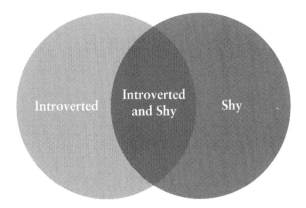

Neither Introverted
nor Shy

How To Tell The Difference Between Introversion And Social Anxiety

Is an introvert simply a person with social anxiety? The short answer is: *nope*.

The slightly longer, but still interesting answer follows.

4 Major Differences between Introversion and Social Anxiety

1. Introversion is a Personality Trait/Social Anxiety is a Disorder

Introversion is a *personality* trait. Or more correctly, an overarching term to describe a collection of mini personality traits. It's biologically based and part of your inherent make-up.

Social anxiety disorder is classified in the Diagnostic and Statistical Manual of Mental Disorders (DSM). Although you may be born with a predisposition to social anxiety, it's learned through experiences and reinforced by avoidance of social situations.

2. Introversion relates to Preference/Social Anxiety relates to Fear

Introversion is marked by a preference for less stimulation — whether people, lights, noise, or other environmental inputs. Introverts are easily over-stimulated and feel uncomfortable, irritable, and uneasy in high-stimulation environments. It's about stimulation, not just about people.

Those at the far end of introversion have a ~~screaming urge~~ strong preference for low-stimulation environments. They may feel a compelling need for quiet, solitude, mental activities, and few social activities. It's not unlike feeling excessively hot all the time, and always needing to turn the temperature down.

People with social anxiety fear social situations. The fear can be debilitating and may significantly interfere with their work, relationships, and quality of life. In fact, social anxiety is also called social phobia, and it's treated therapeutically in a similar way to other phobias.

3. Introversion is about how I feel/Social Anxiety is about what people think of me

When an introvert avoids a social situation, it's so they don't feel the discomfort of excessive stimulation. They may find the noise, lights, people, forced conversations, or combination ~~makes them want to pluck out their own eyeball~~ disturbing and unpleasant. It's like a psychological/neurological version of ants crawling all over you.

When a socially anxious person avoids a social situation, it's to do with fear of how they'll be judged by others. They dread saying or doing something that will cause them embarrassment, humiliation, or rejection.

4. Introversion does not need to be treated/ Social Anxiety may need to be treated

Introverts don't need to be cured or sent away to introvert conversion camp or forced to come out of their shell. Being an introvert is simply a built-in aspect of personality.

Introverts can experiment to find the amount of stimulation that feels right. They can make decisions about how and when to recharge their introvert batteries, how to find balance between solitude and socializing, how to take pleasure in doing things alone, how to adapt to their individual level of introversion — all things we talk about in this book.

People with social anxiety disorder may choose to seek treatment if they're suffering distress. If you think you may be socially anxious, please talk to your doctor.

Introvert or Socially Anxious Person?

To illustrate the difference between introverts and socially anxious people, here are some things an introvert might think:

- I avoid parties. They feel too loud and chaotic.
- I find large group gatherings extremely unpleasant.
- I'm so much happier at home, or having dinner with a close friend, or in a small group.
- I dislike having to come up with conversation on the fly — it feels fake to me.

Here are some things a person with social anxiety might think:

- I'll embarrass myself if I eat in public.
- If I speak to someone new, then they will reject me.
- I'll be humiliated and I won't be able to cope.
- I'm very anxious about what people will think of me.

Which one are you?

You may be an introvert. You may be suffering from social anxiety disorder. You may be both, or neither. As with introversion and shyness, a Venn diagram shows the possibilities:

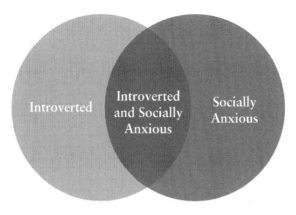

Neither Introverted
nor Socially Anxious

*

The important thing to remember is that you can manage the discomfort of introversion through your choices.

But you should discuss how to treat social anxiety disorder with your doctor.

Part 2: How To Be An Introvert In An Extrovert World

To be yourself in a world that is constantly trying to make you something else is the greatest accomplishment.

—*Ralph Waldo Emerson*

How To Recharge When You're All Peopled Out

If you're an introvert, then you're probably familiar with something I call "introvert overload". It's the feeling that everybody wants a piece of you. The sense that you just can't get enough space from people. The deep, soul-longing for solitude.

I think of it as a kind of "psychological claustrophobia", like the walls are closing in and you Can't. Quite. Breathe.

You might even feel guilty too, because some of the people from whom you want space are your loved ones. Maybe even your spouse. Maybe even — appalled, judgmental gasp — your children.

Seriously, what kind of monster are you? What kind of two-headed, scaly, Satan-beast?

In fact, you are a garden-variety introvert monster. Single-headed, unscaled, 100 percent Satan-free.

You are simply a person who, compared to extroverts, has a higher baseline level of arousal, and uses more mental resources in scanning and processing external stimuli.

Which makes you more sensitive to light, noise, and especially people. Which causes you to become easily overstimulated. Which makes you quick to tire of all the stimulation and desperate to retreat to a sanctuary where you can turn down the psychological volume.

In other words, ~~the monstrosity inside you~~ the way your brain works makes you prone to experience introvert overload.

Introvert Overload: When you ~~hate everybody~~ feel all peopled out

I've become good at recognizing small clues that I'm heading into the throes of introvert overload. Subtle, *tiny* hints give it away.

Like when a stranger comes up and asks me a question without saying "excuse me" and suddenly I'm filled with rage and I begin planning how I might murder them and cleverly dispose of their body. (I'm squeamish so these plans tend to be airbrushed and vague.)

Or if someone tries to do something nice for me but they're in my space while doing the nice thing and mentally I'm saying, *This guy*.

That's when I know I've reached maximum people level and the sirens are screeching and I need to find a way to regain my sense of equanimity.

But how?

What would be cool is if introverts could recharge like the character Seven of Nine on *Star Trek* — just plug in to a Borg alcove and power down and regenerate. No one would be offended. No explanation would be needed. No questions of "What's wrong?" would have to be fielded. We wouldn't feel compelled to apologize for needing what to us is as essential as sleep or air or chocolate.

But where do we introverts find our introvert regeneration alcoves?

Finding your Introvert sanctuary

Extroverts might regenerate with social events, drinks with friends, parties, team sports, adventurous activities, something stimulating. These choices might help them relax, unwind, forget their troubles, feel good.

But for us introverts it can be more complicated. Especially because we can't just *go to* something, we also need to *get away from* people.

Especially if years of being introverts in an extrovert world have made us think we should feel refreshed by going out or hanging with friends. Or doing the things we see other people doing to unwind. Things that only make us crave space *more*.

For example, a while ago I thought a massage would be a good way to refresh myself, so I scheduled an appointment. But the massage dude kept chatting and asking questions, despite my monotone, monosyllabic responses. I spent the whole time clenching everything in an attempt to silently communicate *For the love of Pete PLEASE STOP TALKING*. It was horrendously unrelaxing.

At the end he told me I was very tight and should book in for regular massage appointments so I could loosen up more. Argh!

You wanna go where nobody knows your name

Another odd thing is, when I hit introvert overload and crave space, sometimes I perversely want to be with people — but people who don't want anything from me. People who don't know me and won't make noise around me or ask questions of me or expect any kind of interaction from me. And — as someone who worries about everyone I love — people I don't have to worry about.

And you know where I find these people?

In books and on TV. These are two of my very favorite ways to recharge and feel human again. The relationships I've forged with fictional characters are surprisingly strong. In my head Lorelei Gilmore is and probably always will be my best friend. And I've never really gotten over the loss of the deep and powerful connections I made with the gang in *Buffy*.

What also works for me is nerdy stuff like learning French or art history or doing a crossword.

What all these ways of recharging have in common is they allow me to be alone and enjoy solitude, while also filling my mind with pleasant and engaging distraction so I'm not overthinking or ruminating.

How to recharge if you're an Introvert — Dos and Don'ts

Okay, so how about you? What are some good ways for you to recharge when you're suffering from introvert overload?

Here are some tips …

- Do try to schedule regular introvert-battery-recharging sessions so you always have a little oasis of solitude to look forward to. Maybe one day someone will invent the All-Peopled-Out Safe Word App (see *7 Ingenious Introvert Apps*), but for now you need to be proactive about making time.
- Don't expect conventionally relaxing activities to work for you. Massages, facials, and spa treatments in particular can leave you trapped in a chit-chat vortex from which there's no escape

unless you're prepared to run screaming from the room dressed in paper slippers and a towel.

- Do look for activities that give you pleasure. I complete the crossword each morning while I have breakfast and it's crazy how happy it makes me. You don't just want alone time, you want *pleasurable* alone time.

- Don't leave it too long between mini battery-charging sessions. I read every single night in bed. See the battery-chargers below for ideas for short recharging spells.

- Do negotiate with loved ones for the time you need. I've asked my husband to spend Fridays in his co-share office so I can work at home or do whatever is on my agenda all alone. And ask from a place of self-acceptance, not apology.

- Don't feel guilty. You'll be a happier, calmer, better friend/spouse/parent/relative/workmate when you're no longer feeling overwhelmed and overstimulated from introvert overload.

16 Introvert Battery-Charger Ideas

Here are some ideas you could try:

1. Watch a favorite TV show
2. Listen to an inspiring playlist
3. Treat yourself to your favorite cake at a cafe

4. Write in a pretty notebook
5. Plan a goal or project
6. Listen to an audiobook
7. Do a crossword puzzle
8. People-watch at a cafe
9. Go to a movie by yourself
10. Take a drive and sing along with the radio
11. Sip coffee or tea while appreciating a moment alone
12. Do a mindfulness practice
13. Feel grateful
14. Learn something
15. Read a novel
16. Go for a walk

How To Come Out As An Introvert

I guess at some level I always knew that I was ... different.

Sure, I experimented during my younger years. Even though I'd heard it would make you go blind, I did it constantly. Reading, that is. And coming up with dubious excuses to avoid parties and stay in. And lurking in places where others like me hung out (libraries).

It's just a phase, I would tell myself. Eventually I'll grow out of it and be like everybody else.

Like the people in movies and TV shows. Shiny, happy people. Socially active, big-group people.

At school and while studying for my first degree (commerce) it was easy to hang out in small, close groups. To eschew parties and frequent socializing and just keep a low profile.

But when I started working in large financial institutions, it became harder to fit in. So many people. Endless meetings. So much talking. Constant get-togethers. Open-plan offices where I could never concentrate and would have to stay late every night to get my work done after people went home. Bright overhead fluorescents that flickered interminably. People always chattering, buzzing around, so much energy, so much confidence. Talk talk talk. People people *PEOPLE*.

How could I be so young and feel so utterly exhausted? What the hell was my problem?

I'd Rather be Fishing (and I hate Fishing)

I remember a team-building weekend when I worked at a large investment bank. It was held at a lovely resort on the water, my suite was gorgeous, the food was fabulous. Yet I was in introvert hell.

After a day of ice-breakers and group activities, another girl and I swiped a bottle of champagne and escaped from the evening's socializing to join some fishermen who'd invited us onto their little boat. We just sat and sipped, the fishermen fished, it was quiet.

Our colleagues were not happy. And I understood that; part of me knew why they were judging us. But I simply couldn't go back until it was quiet again and I could creep into the peace of my room. I lay in the dark sensing my colleagues' disdain and wondering … What the hell was my problem?

There's Something Wrong with this Fantasy

During my time in corporate life I had a couple of excellent bosses, great opportunities, challenging work I enjoyed and was good at, and I was very well paid. Which is probably how I managed to last as long as I did — about 13 years.

And the thing is, I desperately wanted a corporate career — or thought I did. Now when I look back I wonder if it was because in my formative years the only females in pop culture who *did* things, rather than simply nagging or being a sidekick or needing to be rescued, were corporate high flyers. In those days we had no *Buffy* or *Veronica Mars* to show that a girl could be the hero of her own life in her own way. I wanted to be a girl who did stuff, and in those days the girls who did stuff did career stuff.

Either that, or it was the little business suits with the big shoulders that enticed me to a corporate career. Yeah, possibly it was the cute suits.

Anyway, eventually the signs that something was wrong grew more insistent. One day I was chatting with a friend and mentioned a fantasy I'd have when returning to work after lunch.

> "You know, when you fantasize about getting hit by a car, so you don't have to go back? Not a lot, just enough to land you in hospital for a few weeks?"

Her eyes widened. "No, I do not have that fantasy," she said slowly.

Hmmm. OK then. So what the hell was my problem?

Corners of Shame

I guess the look on her face sank in, because not long after that I left my job. My department was undergoing yet another restructure that would have me reporting to someone I didn't respect. I took that as a sign to get out and asked to be made redundant.

During my outplacement I was put through the usual battery of psych tests. The psychologist who wrote my report took me aside one afternoon and said, "I've never seen someone less well suited to this kind of corporate culture. How have you stayed so long and not had a nervous breakdown?"

Whoa. It was one of those defining moments. It started to dawn on me that maybe it wasn't *me* who was wrong, maybe I was just in the wrong place. Square. Peg.

But what was the nature of my squareness? What precisely did the others have that I lacked? What made up my corners, made me nervous-breakdown-able in this environment?

After leaving corporate life I went back to school and did a psych degree — something I'd always wanted to do — and it was there I found my answers.

Weirdness, Thy Name is Introversion

While I was studying the subjects of psychometrics (psych testing) and personality theory, two things became clear.

First, as we discussed earlier in *How To Understand The Psychology Of Introverts*, one of five aspects of personality that are pretty intrinsic to who we are and how we navigate the world is extroversion/introversion. This is how easily we're stimulated by people, noise, lights and external input. Neither is better than the other, although extroversion is certainly more visible in movies, the media, and pop culture — perhaps leading introverts to feel like the odd ones.

Second, I am at the extreme end of introversion. You know the long tail? I'm in that triangular bit on the end.

In light of these discoveries, a cascade of memories came tumbling over me and got reinterpreted and reprocessed, exactly like that scene in *The Sixth Sense*. It's a pretty significant epiphany to realize you've been misjudging yourself, and Bruce Willis, for a long, long time.

There's no Avoidr for Introverts

At first, my attempts to embrace the introvert lifestyle were tentative. There's no starter app for introverts (Avoidr?) to help you along. And anyway, introverts would probably never use the options to chat or connect, so I'm not sure how it would actually work.

But as I came to embrace my inner (and outer) introvert, I learned a lot.

- I learned that turning up begrudgingly to gatherings *you* have organized is best avoided by not actually organizing such gatherings in the first place.
- I learned that you can bypass the 5 stages of canceling plans (see *How To Recognize The 5 Stages Of Canceling Plans*) by sending a gracious decline early on.
- I learned that good friends invite you to their parties, send a sweet note saying you don't have to come, and then make a separate quiet date with you (my friends are really this awesome).
- I learned that genuine conversation with close friends is the best.
- I learned that TV shows are a fabulous way to feel like you're spending time with people without feeling like you have to be "on".
- I learned that, for me, no amount of money is enough to justify working in a corporate career.

- I learned that once you stop worrying about not being an extrovert, there's a lot of pleasure in being an introvert — a happiness in your own company, a delight in books, crossword puzzles, TV shows, thinking, planning, creating, learning, ideas, or however you like to ~~be a nerd~~ do your introverting.

My Introvert Lifestyle

Over time I've also made a bunch of decisions and trade-offs to have a lifestyle that makes me happier, and therefore a better wife, relative, and friend.

- I start the day with breakfast alone while I do the crossword.
- I work in my apartment, in a quiet home-office. I get more done and do better work than I was ever capable of in an open-plan space.
- I manage my schedule with care, generally limiting myself to no more than one or two social dates a week.
- Every few weeks I schedule a weekend with no social plans at all.
- If I start to feel overwhelmed and peopled-out I take an afternoon off to binge-watch TV and eat junk food.
- I keep a big pile of books by my bed — fiction, humor, memoir, biography — so there's always

something to match my mood. And I read every night before falling asleep.

These days I love being an introvert and get a kick out of laughing at my idiosyncrasies.

And I've stopped asking, *So what the hell is my problem*. I've realized there isn't one.

How To Be Introvert-ish (Hint: There Are No Pure Introverts Or Extroverts)

Some people just know they're introverts. If, like me, you're at the extreme end of introversion, then you know it. If you're reading this book and saying, *That is so me!* but quietly and to yourself, then you know it.

But what if it's not so clear? What if you feel kinda introvert-y? Could you be introvert-adjacent?

Being Introvert-ish

Yes, you could, and here's why. In fact two whys.

First, extroversion/introversion is not an either/or switch where you are simply one or the other. You will fall somewhere on the spectrum between pure extroversion and pure introversion — toward one end or the other, or in the middle, or leaning in one direction.

Second, as we saw earlier in *How To Understand The Psychology Of Introverts*, extroversion/introversion is a pretty broad concept that actually encompasses a number of narrower traits — including level of sociability, energy, activity, sensation-seeking, interpersonal dominance, and tendency to experience positive emotional states.

You might be high on some of these finer traits and low on others. Or in the middle on some and more extreme on others.

All this variability can leave you feeling part introvert, part extrovert, part ambivert (no, not like a salamander — you're thinking of amphibian). Or part pseutrovert. Okay, I made that last one up, but I've talked to a number of people who aren't introverted yet feel connected to the *idea* of being an introvert, and I think that's a good word for them.

To show you examples of the various shades of introverts, extroverts, and ambiverts out there, here are some of my real-life friends*.

*These are my real friends but not their real names — though I think these names are actually better.

Examples of Introverts, Extroverts, and Ambiverts

Candastasia

Candastasia is always doing a million things. She adores having people drop in unexpectedly. She craves adventure and her holidays often involve something wild or off the beaten track. Her business is run with so many balls in the air that she barely needs a floor. She is spontaneous, open, and gregarious. She talks fast and with incredible passion. She is dizzyingly energetic. She enjoys being a leader and has a naturally strong, dominant style. Just thinking about her makes me want to have a little lie-down. She would be high on most of the aspects of extroversion.

Kryptonia

In many ways, Kryptonia is a classic, people-person extrovert. She is sociable, extremely popular, always busy, energetic, easygoing, positive. When we used to work together she'd hold the lift door open for everybody — and then chat with them all! (I would desperately avert my eyes and will the doors to hurry up and close.) She lives on an estate with a strong community and heaps of interaction with neighbors — and she loves it. As a mother of two young boys she doesn't often get a night to herself, but when she does, there's nothing she enjoys more than going out with some of her exuberant, fun-loving friends. Yet Kryptonia is also extremely organized and enjoys order and routine, something you might not associate with the more extroverted temperament. When she and I have dinner there's no small talk and lots of intimate conversation, often to the point of scaring our waiter.

Wontonio

In true extrovert style, Wontonio loves being the center of attention. He is smart, charismatic, funny, entertaining, and excellent company. He is more open and consistently himself than anyone I've ever met. His sensation-seeking leads him to love bungee jumping and all kinds of crazy (to me) adventures. He is comfortable with levels of uncertainty that would leave me weeping in a fetal position in the corner. But every so often he has episodes of extreme introversion, where he disengages from social media and social life and withdraws into himself to recharge. He's not depressed; he finds this downtime pleasurable — like a hibernation that gets him ready for re-emerging in the spring.

Suspira

Suspira is one of those wonderful connectors who knows lots of people and is great at putting the right people in touch with each other. She is outgoing and friendly, loves learning new things, and enjoys a high level of mental and social stimulation in her life. Although an extrovert in many ways, she is aware of needing to batten down her social hatches regularly. She used to find this need for social downtime at odds with what she thought was a straightforward extrovert personality. But, like most people, her personality is more complex, and since understanding she's probably more of an ambivert, she's better able to recognize when she needs to recharge her social battery.

Allabasta

When Allabasta and I studied psychology together I was in awe of her energy and ability to be good at many diverse things and get things done without fuss or over-analysis (how was that even possible?). She had lots of extracurricular activities and an extremely active social life. Nowadays though, as the mother of twin toddler boys, her emotional and social energy is very different. Because the demands of twins means she sometimes has to say no to things, she's discovered how good it feels to do less, and how much happier she feels when she respects this introverted part of herself. Her confidence blinded her to her introverted tendencies and masked her underlying preferences, but recognizing she's an undercover introvert has brought her greater peace and a helpful lens through which to view her relationships.

Lilithia

Lilithia is quiet and reserved, and at first I thought she was an introvert. But she really enjoys socializing and entertaining and even being onstage teaching fitness classes. In fact, she's somewhat extroverted and shy, rather than introverted. When in a class together, I notice everything — what people are wearing/who's out of time/what the guy outside the studio is doing — while she easily tunes it all out. Like many extroverts with their lower arousal levels, she is miraculously (to me) good at ignoring things she is not interested in. I want that ability!

Which One are You?

Does it matter where you fall on the introvert — ambivert — extrovert spectrum? Not in terms of having a pointless label, nope. Where it is helpful is in understanding yourself, your preferences, your personality.

In particular, if you have introvert tendencies, then recognizing and respecting them can make a big difference to your life. Because that self-knowledge helps you better manage your time, energy, work, social life, and intimate relationships.

All of which makes you a happier introvert, extrovert, or ambivert.

How To Stop Being A Faux Extrovert And Find Your Social Sweet Spot

I was a Faux Extrovert

Like many readers of this book, I spent much of my adult life as a "faux extrovert". What do I mean by that?

I went out more than I wanted. Every weekend, because that's what people do. Whenever someone asked, because, um, they asked.

I made more small talk than felt right. Chatted ad nauseam about things I could not care less about. Ignored my own longing to discuss what was really happening in our lives and debriefed endless nothings instead.

I talked on the phone more than was comfortable. It would be rude to ignore the call, thoughtless not to call back. I came to loathe the sound of a ringing telephone.

Now let me be clear. I'm not saying there's anything wrong with going out a lot, or any particular topic of conversation, or chatting on the phone. What I am saying is that there was something wrong with my being *so out of touch with my own needs*. So clueless about what felt right to me, what energized and drained and made me happy. So unwilling to factor my desires into the mix. So controlled by other people's preferences.

And because I constantly ignored myself to fit in and play the faux extrovert, I felt exhausted and overwhelmed and irritable and misanthropic.

A Series of Unfortunate Minor Electrocutions

I also got sick a lot, in what I now see was my body's way of saying I CANNOT DO THIS ANYMORE. Being sick was an acceptable excuse for escaping the incessant people-ness of work. For turning down invitations or staying home at the weekend. For canceling plans when I felt all peopled-out and incapable of putting on the mask and doing the being-with-people dance.

It would make a better story to say I had one lightning-bolt transformational moment when everything changed, but it was more a series of small electric shocks. I was Homer Simpson-like in my ability to get zapped and say *D'oh* and just stick my finger idiotically back into the power point. The shocks singed my hair and burned my skin until finally one day I found myself wondering *Where the hell did my eyebrows go*?

Now don't laugh, but I'm going to outline the utter depth of my density in not getting the introvert thing.

Introvert Denial 1: Cubicle Fatigue

At school and university, I hung out with just a few close friends. I enjoyed reading and watching DVDs for relaxation. I spent a lot of time alone just doing my own nerdy thing. When I moved out of home it was to a tiny one-bedroom apartment by myself.

But I didn't realize I was an introvert.

My first job was in a small company with my own office where I got my work done in peace. I loved it. But it was the start of the 90s and the only females in pop culture who were neither sidekicks, nags, nor victims were corporate high flyers. So I decided to take my enormous shoulder pads and big hair and try my luck in the corporate jungle.

But alas, I didn't realize I was an ill-suited introvert.

After personality testing for a role at a fancy-schmancy investment bank I was told I was too introverted for their open-plan, super-confident, hyper-social culture. *That's absurd!* I exclaimed — but silently, in my own mind. Aloud I gently convinced them I was the confident extrovert I desperately wished to be, and got the job, and was promptly absolutely miserable. Before too long I left the big salary and perks and took a huge pay-cut to return to a small company.

But I didn't realize it was because I was an introvert.

Still longing to be a chick who did shit and still lacking any model of what that looked like, I ventured back to corporate life, with its open-plan, high-flying, extrovert-a-go-go culture — also known as introvert hell. I had a great boss and CEO, plus work I enjoyed and was good at, which made it hard to face the fact that the incessant people-ness was a terrible fit for my personality.

Corporate nastiness was the straw that made me request redundancy for me and my camel.

But *still* I didn't realize how much my career had been affected by this introvert thing.

The Introvert Lens

Extricated from corporate life, I did a psychology degree and discovered I was at the distant-horizon end of introversion. That was a major revelation. (You're starting to question whether I should be allowed to walk among normal humans, aren't you?) Still, I didn't understand *how much* this revelation explained. It seemed like a label, not a fundamental lens through which I could make sense of my life.

But something began to penetrate the sheer rock of my brain, because I did my thesis on "Personality and Happiness" — a topic then disdained (happiness wasn't yet considered a legitimate field of study). And when it was time to choose my psych career, the little part of me that had been putting things together over the years woke up and smelled the coffee and screamed — DO NOT BECOME A CLINICAL PSYCHOLOGIST OR YOU WILL SURELY DIE OF TOO MUCH PEOPLE.

So instead I logged onto the internet and tapped away on my keyboard and started writing, which is where I've been ever since.

Introvert Denial 2: Nasal Emissions

Although I'd found work that suited my introverted disposition, I still struggled socially. Because, you know, I only had decades of experiences and a psych degree and a thesis on the topic to guide me. *Sheesh*.

Anyway, the final piece of the puzzle — a puzzle most five-year-olds would have solved, spilled juice over, and fallen asleep on by now — came just a few years ago when I had surgery on my nose so I could sleep better. (My nose basically had to be broken and reconstructed to correct narrow passages, enlarged turbinates, and a deviated septum.) For three months I had to rest.

Those three months were eye-opening. Though often I had to keep my eyes closed because of the cast and the splints. But *internally* I was seeing things for the first time. Externally I also saw things for the first time, but they were mostly gross things because that's what comes out of your nose when you have rhinal surgery.

Anyway. I was literally *not allowed to go out.* It was a Get-out-of-Jail-Free card, the introvert equivalent of *calorie-free chocolate*. It was like angels singing. Probably something from the 80s — I'm thinking Human League, possibly Duran Duran. It was sweet and heavenly and full of synth sounds and joyful keyboards.

Finally I had an excuse to say no to social engagements. A medically justified reason for staying in. And you know what that did? *It showed me how it felt to do less.* It gave me a taste of what it was like lower down the socializing scale. It helped me get in touch with my "people sweet-spot", which I'd never felt entitled to explore before. It let me find my "introvert equilibrium".

Finding my Introvert Equilibrium

Now if you're still sorting out how to be an introvert in an extrovert world, then I'm not suggesting you get nose surgery. Or change careers. Hopefully you're less dense than I've been and even if not, you have this book to save you a lot of time and cubicle-fatigue, and honestly some pretty gross nasal effusions.

Here are a few of the lessons I learned. Eventually. Um, like *eventually* eventually.

1. I only go out socially on Saturday nights and sometimes Tuesday nights. Any more than this and I go into introvert overload.
2. I plan a weekend-in every few weeks and put it in my diary as a date. There's usually binge-watching of Netflix or Nordic Noir and major snacking involved. It feels like a mini-vacation and I really look forward to it.
3. I schedule gym classes in my diary as commitments, and these preclude work meetings or social dates (except of course emergencies). This helps me feel balanced.
4. I have one-on-one friend dates with my closest friends — usually dinner, or wine and cheese, over which we can really talk, laugh, and share. This satisfies my need for meaning and depth and lets me be a good, present friend to my most cherished buddies. Oh — and I always wear something nice to make it feel special.
5. My husband and I have couple friends that we see together and individual friends and groups that we see separately. This gives us both time at home alone (which one of us may spend singing

loudly to 80s hits) as well as time to be our individual selves with friends.

6. I generally avoid parties and organized events unless it's really important to someone I care about.

Finding your People Sweet-Spot

I don't know what's right for you. But if you're still processing how to be a happy, well-balanced introvert, then you may need to experiment to find your people sweet-spot.

You don't have to be the gregarious and social being that's often seen as the picture of a happy, well-adjusted person. Being a faux extrovert like this can leave you cranky and anxious. If this is where you are now, then give yourself permission to do less, go out less, socialize less. And see how that feels.

On the other hand, you probably should avoid going full-on Walden and retreating to a cabin in the woods from where you pen your solitary scratchings. Most of us, even introverts, need social interaction and enjoy giving and receiving friendship. You may need to give yourself a small push to leave your hermitage and spend quality, meaningful time with the people who matter in your life, but you will likely be happier for it.

So it's a matter of tuning in to how you feel, turning the people-dial a little up or down, and seeing how that new level feels. Of experimenting until you find your people sweet-spot. If you're like me, you'll find it easier to manage this balance if you have a routine like the one I've outlined above. And if you're like me, you'll also have great taste in music so you've got that going on as well.

But do let yourself explore to find your own people sweet-spot. You'll feel less cranky and more happy, and you'll be a better, calmer friend.

How To Enjoy The Pleasure Of Doing Things Alone

My husband Craig and I recently took my mother out for dinner. At the table beside us was a woman dining by herself. I noticed her, partly because I don't often see someone having dinner alone. Breakfast or lunch at a cafe with eyes glued to a phone, yes. But dinner at a somewhat fancy restaurant? Not often. And partly because, if it's in the human visual or auditory spectrum, I'll notice it, overanalyze it, and form elaborate and probably upsetting theories about it.

I tried to watch her discreetly out of the corner of my eye, which more than once caused the waiter to come over and check everything was okay. Presumably I looked like I was on the verge of a medical episode. She, however, was having a perfectly fine evening — enjoying her food, her wine, her own company.

It got me thinking about the supposed stigma of doing things alone. Not just at-home things like reading and watching TV and hiding when unexpected visitors knock. But *out-there* things.

As introverts we're easily overstimulated and distracted by other people and generally happy with our own company, so it makes sense we enjoy doing things alone.

But are we concerned about what other people think? Do we feel embarrassed to be seen dining alone, or going to a concert or lecture by ourselves, or taking a trip solo? Are we discouraged from doing things we're interested in because we don't want people to judge us, or feel sorry for us?

This is what being Happily Alone looks like

Perhaps the single happiest day of my life was a long one spent entirely alone at CERN, the European Organization for Nuclear Research. I went to lectures, took a tour of the Large Hadron Collider (this was before it was completed, not a ride on a super-fast, teeny-tiny rollercoaster or anything), had fascinating conversations with the scientists (I even got offered a job!), and wandered for hours through the exhibitions. Multiple, screaming (but you know, *quiet*) nerdgasms.

More mundanely, I always go shopping alone — it's more efficient and less distracting and there's nobody to say *Don't you already have a lot of wine at home?* or *Are you sure having a "back-up" espresso machine is a thing?* And I used to go to the movies alone every week (though these days I prefer the writing of shows on TV).

I usually attend art exhibitions with Craig but we separate as soon as we get there. He goes through quickly and then finds a cafe where he reads and waits for me. I view everything three times: first to gain an overview, second to peruse in detail, third to scan and get the big picture. I've attended dozens of lectures, courses, and classes by myself — on art, cosmology, serial killers, literature, and screen-writing. (I did one three-day seminar three times without ever once talking to another attendee, and it was amazing.)

I enjoy activities more when I can do them at my own strange pace and in my own nerdy way and can process them *without being attentive to another person's experience.* It's simply less tiring and more pleasurable.

Cultivate Introvert Self-Acceptance before worrying what others think

I never feel embarrassed to be out on my own — except for those times I forget I'm in public and belt out a horrendously off-key line from the song in my earbuds. Usually, thanks to several years cultivating a strong sense of self-acceptance about being an introvert, I simply don't care what strangers think of me. I have a strong line between people whose opinions matter and people whose opinions I cannot worry myself about.

And it's been my experience that the more I accept myself and my introvert ways, the more others respect me. I felt much more judged by others when I judged myself.

So I'd like to encourage you, if you're avoiding doing activities or pursuing interests on your own because you're concerned what others might think of you, to challenge that concern. To deliberately cultivate self-acceptance and nurture disregard for other people's judgments. You cannot expect everyone to understand your introvert ways — and as soon as you give up trying, you'll find it easier to live a happy, fulfilling introvert life.

I'm grateful to that woman for happily dining by herself the other night. She inspired me.

And I hope she also inspires you, if you need inspiration, to enjoy the pleasure of doing things alone.

How To Cope When People Tell You To "Come Out Of Your Shell"

If you're an introvert then there's a good chance you've had at least one of these phrases said to you. Probably many of them. Probably many times.

- You should come out of your shell.
- You need to put yourself out there.
- You ought to make more friends.
- You're so boring.
- Why do you hate people?
- What's wrong?/Are you okay?
- Why are you in a bad mood?/Are you depressed?
- Come out — we'll cheer you up.
- You overthink/overanalyze everything.
- You ought to get out of the house more.
- You're too sensitive.
- You should smile more.
- Why are you so quiet?/Why don't you talk more?
- It's not healthy to spend so much time alone.
- You need to try harder/come out of your comfort zone/change.

And, based on the responses when I asked about such comments on the Louder Minds Facebook Page, you are absolutely fed up with hearing them.

So what can you do? How should you respond?

Well, carefully, is my advice. Because, for one thing, the people who make these comments are often speaking out of love or concern about you.

For another, explaining introversion to a non-introvert is not easy. It's a bit like explaining chocolate to a person without taste buds: it can be very frustrating and somehow in the process you end up eating a lot of chocolate.

With that in mind, here are a few steps for dealing with advice from well-meaning friends and loved ones.

Not Depressed, not Lonely, just INTROVERTED

Step 1. Accept yourself first

Accepting yourself is the single most important thing you can do to convince others that you are fine as you are.

If you judge yourself harshly, compare yourself unfairly to more gregarious people, apologize for your preferences, feel inadequate because you dislike parties and enjoy your own company (what a monster!), then other people are going to pick up on it.

But if instead you accept that being an introvert is part of you; if you allow yourself to take absolute pleasure in this, to relish your time alone and your solitary pursuits *instead of feeling embarrassed by them*; if you cultivate a sense of joy in the geeky/quiet/reserved aspect of yourself — then that will come across too.

How can you nurture this self-acceptance?

If you like to journal, begin to write about the simple pleasures of your introvert life. *Dear Diary, today I spent time with me. It was ever so dreamy.*

If you like to talk, discuss these joys with a good friend. No, not a bottle-of-wine-friend, a *person*-friend. Though maybe bottle-friend can join you both.

If you practice mindfulness, become aware of how great it feels to engage in your work and hobbies and interests and geeky pursuits. *Breathing in: I am surrounded by books and the remote and snacks. Breathing out: I am happy.*

However you do it, consciously *enjoy* your introvert pleasures — and *feel* your enjoyment! The more you allow yourself to appreciate your own unique experience of life, the less other people will worry about you — or if they do, the less you'll let it bother you.

Step 2. Pick your battles

One of the happy side effects of accepting yourself is an instant, dramatic reduction in your concern about what other people think of you.

Of course there'll be true friends and loved ones who matter, and with whom you'll want to have a deeper conversation, as we'll discuss in the next step.

But for the most part, you'll simply cease to care about being misjudged or misunderstood by the majority of advice givers. It's very unlikely you'll change their view, and life's too short to try. *This is incredibly liberating.* One of the major epiphanies of my adult life has been realizing that it's actually okay to be misunderstood. Letting go of defending yourself saves so much energy.

For these people, dealing with unwanted advice can be as simple as:

- Using humor:
  You know I don't just have one shell, right? I have a whole *closet* full of shells. But I think this one brings out my eyes.
- Saying thanks: (with a smile and maybe a squeeze of the hand)
  I appreciate that you care about me.
- Changing the subject:
  Speaking of (something you weren't speaking of at all), let me now introduce a complete non-sequitur …

- Turning the tables:
  It's so funny you should say that, because I was thinking you go out too much. What are your thoughts on that? (You need to be able to do this with a wink and a smile or it could backfire.)
- Streamlining your friendships:
  Introverts tend to be happier with fewer, deeper friendships. Be prepared to spend more of your limited energy on fewer people who matter to you more.

Step 3. Come out as an Introvert

For the people in your life who matter to you, it's worth explaining a little about what it's like to be an introvert. Because for them, especially people at the high end of extroversion, doing the things we do with their personality make-up *would* be depressing. They would be miserable!

Remember that just as we are easily *overstimulated*, which *we* find extremely uncomfortable, extroverts are easily *under-stimulated*, which *they* find extremely uncomfortable. They know how bad *they* would feel if they behaved as we do — staying home, having solitary interests, being quiet — and they want to save us from that.

By helping them understand that what makes us happy is different, that we enjoy different things, we can reassure them that they don't have to worry about us, or try to change us, or keep giving us advice.

So how can you have this conversation? You could share your own "coming out as an introvert" story. Or give them this book. Or let your loved ones ask any questions that come up for them.

Being Happy in Your Way

Sadly, especially for those of us who like to be in control and would make an excellent Queen Of The World (just saying), you can't change other people. And the more you rail against people's annoying habits, the more you set them in place.

But by changing *yourself* you can change the dynamic in a relationship, and that often causes the other person to change as well.

If you're fed up with unwanted advice from people who don't understand your introvert ways, look first at your own behavior. Make sure you're setting the standard with your own self-acceptance. This is absolutely crucial, and on its own, will transform your relationship with yourself and with others. A lot of your concern about other people's opinions will fall away, and you'll be able to be deal with their advice more lightly, with humor, with kindness.

And for the people in your life who really matter, the ones who deserve a real conversation, you'll have the energy, and I'm hoping this book will give you the resources, to understand each other better. And to let each other be happy in their own way.

How To Embrace Minimalism

Not long ago I experienced some of the most stressful weeks of my life. Even if I hadn't been feeling the effects via poor sleep and a general sense of bleurgh, I could measure it by that universal stress barometer — quantity of chocolate consumed. I find chocolate therapy, where you discuss your feelings with, say, a plate of chocolate-chip cookies, to be highly effective. No judgment. Unconditional chocolate. Or love. Which is the same thing, really.

Anyway, those weeks were an introvert's nightmare.

It all began when we decided to sell our apartment. Because of several factors — spring being a good time, advice from property people, a complete failure to take reality into account — we decided to do it very quickly.

Thus ensued a head-spinning maelstrom of tradespeople to paint, re-carpet, change tapware, complete repairs, clean, spruce, refresh, style, photograph, and generally transform our apartment into a sparkling, updated version of itself. You can just picture the makeover montage with upbeat soundtrack, right?

Much of this process was horrible for my home-loving, easily overwhelmed, extreme-introvert personality — strangers traipsing through my home, unbelievable amounts of mess left by tradespeople, countless decisions to be made, endless costs, numerous phone calls, disruption to routines and comforts, paint fumes, allergic reactions to cleaning products (I came out in three separate rashes), poor sleep, physical exhaustion.

There was also the added stress of wondering whether people attending the open inspections were peeking inside my cupboards and judging me for my apocalypse-ready stashes of chocolate, sweet potato crisps and wine.

But amid the awfulness, one thing emerged as a delight. No, *more* than that. One thing brought a joy that is profound and unhyperbolically life-changing.

That one thing was stripping down our possessions.

I'd been wanting to declutter for a while, but something about the idea of leaving this apartment where we'd lived for nearly two decades made me go extreme. I didn't just get rid of surplus stuff, unworn clothes, and busted appliances. I released entire "lifestyles" — whole classes of things, complete suites of furniture and everything that went inside them.

And through the process I had several epiphanies that convinced me I was doing the right thing. Here were my four lightbulb moments.

Epiphany 1: We only need stuff for the life we want to live

What do I mean by that?

For example, we had stuff for the "lifestyle" where we entertained.

When we were first married and I was still caught in the trap of doing things I thought were expected of me, we entertained a lot. This required multiple ranges of glassware, mugs, crockery, serving dishes, different-sized bowls, napery, a large buffet to store it all in, and most of all, an ability to spend hours at a time gritting my teeth and internally screaming.

But now we entertain rarely, and when we do have people over it's casual and our everyday stuff is quite lovely and perfectly suitable.

Craig drinks Scotch and I drink ~~great vats of~~ a very occasional red wine and these are the only special-purpose glassware we need.

So that other life … gone. *puff*

I also had stuff for the "lifestyle" where I was a businessperson. I am literally yawning as I type this.

I had business books and folders of notes from training courses. I had uptight little outfits suitable for business events. I had a Herman Miller built-in work-station that was so cubicle-esque you could almost hear the pointy-haired boss talking about deliverables going forward. Totally corporate-looking. Totally not-me.

These were all vestiges of the days when I thought I was a businessperson who wrote. But over the years I've realized I'm a writer wanting to make a living from my words.

Now I learn things as I need to know them. I have outfits that are relaxed but perfectly fine for the occasional business thing I attend. I have a desk that suits me and feels more like a creative workspace and less like a Dilbert cube.

So that other life ... happily, joyfully gone. *puff*

Epiphany 2: Keeping things for later stops me acting now

Another epiphany I had during my declutter was this: saving things for later stops me getting their benefit now.

For example: books. As I read, I used to highlight good ideas and dog-ear important things to act on. But in all my decades of reading books and high-lighting and dog-earing, *I have never gone back and looked through these reminders.*

And there's something more. The idea that I can go back later? That stops me doing anything *now.*

By keeping the book for action *one day*, I let myself get away with changing nothing *today*.

Now, I'm already reading differently. If I see something I want to look up, or do, or whatever, I make a note on a Post-It. In the morning (I read at night in bed) I stick the Post-It in my diary and it becomes a to-do item immediately.

Now, once I've finished a book, I will actually be finished with the book. That feels … different. And lighter.

Hmmm, the present. It's a place I'm hoping to spend a lot more time.

Epiphany 3: I will need some of this stuff, but I don't know what

As I released so much stuff from our home, I started to worry we might need things I was jettisoning with gay abandon. By which I mean, with hairbrush microphone in hand and Gloria Gaynor playing loudly in the background.

Until I had my third ~~glass of red~~ epiphany.

Of course we'd need some of these things. No doubt about it. That tall vase or the really long extension cord or whatever. But when I thought about it, I figured there might be, say, ten things we'd miss. *Only we couldn't know which ten items they'd be.*

And that realization made the choice easy …

Would I rather keep *all* this stuff for the few things I would need again, or simply buy those particular ten items as they were needed?

Would I rather pay for storage — both in physical terms of needing more space, as well as psychological clutter — or pay for occasional replacement items?

So all the stuff has now gone. I'm curious to see which items we end up missing — and happy to enjoy all the extra physical and mental space in the meantime.

Epiphany 4: The world has changed — time to catch up

I had the most organized, tidy, color-coded filing system. But I created it in the days when the only way to look something up was to go through your paper statements. You guys, I'm talking about pre-internet!

This antediluvian method of keeping records required a most heinous monstrosity of ugliness: a filing cabinet. *shudder*

So I extracted the really important documents — wills, passports, insurance policies, plus tasting notes on a recent wine purchase, obviously. I banished the remaining reams of paper-cuts-in-waiting to be recycled or shredded. I set free the filing cabinet to blight some other poor person's home.

We also had shelves of CDs and DVDs. A few were rescued — my boxed sets of art documentaries, some beloved DVDs of Craig's — but in an age of Netflix and iTunes, the rest could be let go.

Books have been harder. I've not made the transition to ereader and I'm one of those people who gets tactile pleasure and psychological comfort from the look and feel and smell of books. We had a beautiful set of bookcases, an entire wall of books — now we've each kept only the books we're currently reading and a few more that are special.

The loss of all our books has been sad. But my new present-focused approach to reading has made this easier, too.

With the cloud and streaming and everything online, it makes good sense to only keep physical versions of the essentials. Much easier to search for things, too.

The Joy of Less

As an introvert I'm easily overstimulated and I've always taken pleasure in simplicity and minimalism. But this radical declutter was on another level — it's brought so much joy and been like a balm for my soul.

And the four epiphanies I've described made it a simple decision to pare down our possessions to a fraction of what they were.

We now take pleasure in opening closets and cup-boards and seeing ... space. Of having fewer pieces of furniture because there's so much less to put in and on them.

But even more wonderful than the liberated space has been the psychological benefits ...

The shifting more into the present moment. That's kind of freaked me out, in a good way.

The letting go of formats that are out of date. That has felt truly liberating.

The giving up of lifestyles, or rather the accoutrement of lifestyles, that just aren't who we are anymore. That has been nothing short of a thrill.

If you've been thinking about simplifying your life, of going minimal, then I encourage you to take the step.

Especially if you're an easily overwhelmed introvert, you will feel liberated by less. I promise — you will feel *joy*. I hope my four epiphanies help you along the way.

How To Embrace Depth

I've always been impressed by people who can juggle a million things. Confident multi-taskers. High flyers with numerous projects in train and tons of friends on rotation and what looks like a wildly exciting life.

But since discovering I'm an introvert and embracing my personal weirdness I've realized that's simply not me. I'm more of a minimalist juggler. The kind of juggler who can handle one ball, maybe two. *Maybe.*

I suspect it's related to the introvert tendency to feel easily overstimulated, easily overwhelmed.

Now I see it as a considerable strength. I may not be able to handle a lot at once, but I can go deep. I can concentrate and get pretty good at something. I can sustain momentum.

Here are some of the ways I've opted to go deep rather than broad in my life. In every case I've found this minimalist approach a calmer, more effective, happier way to live.

Friendship

In my younger days I used to go out whenever I was invited and be friends with whoever asked. I didn't know it was an option not to. As a result I was chronically, profoundly, brain-crunchingly *all peopled out*.

I now have a handful of close friends, and my time with them is one-on-one or in small groups, usually over drinks or dinner. Hardly ever at functions or parties.

Because of this *social minimalism*, my friendships all grow over time. We get to know each other and ourselves better, we talk about important things, we learn from and are challenged by one another. It's not uncommon for me to still be thinking about dinner conversations days or weeks later. And not because I'm only just getting the jokes. Though okay, yeah, that too.

There's nothing wrong with having large circles of friends or enjoying parties — if that's you. If it's not, it's a great relief to give them up for fewer friends and quieter times. As a bonus, some very good wine is often discovered in the process.

Social Media

When you're a writer you feel pressure to be on every social media platform. Certainly the latest ones where apparently *everybody* is. Definitely those cool ones where that thing you don't really understand is happening, like, *big time.*

I feel the pressure for sure, but I've chosen to take a minimalist approach and focus mostly on my blog, Facebook, and Instagram.

No doubt I miss out on potential audiences by limiting my social media channels. But the stress and faint sense of desperation I feel when I extend myself further on social media is not worth it to me. Much better to be authentic and sane with fewer followers and readers.

Like you!

Hobbies

There are so many things I'm interested in, so many hobbies I'd like to cultivate. I'm a polymath without the actual learning. Just a poly I guess.

I'd love to take up ballroom dancing again, be able to draw, master calligraphy, learn interior design, do a fine arts course, get a degree in science. I want to subscribe to *Vogue Living* and *The New Yorker* and *New Scientist* and read every issue. I have a secret desire to be able to play "Morning Has Broken" on the piano like in the Cat Stevens version.

But I know from experience, from money wasted on courses unfinished and subscriptions unread, that

I end up feeling pressured when I try to do or learn too many things. Even things I love.

So each year I pick just a couple of interests to focus on. Last year it was French (I worked through the entire Rosetta Stone course) and art history (I watched a bunch of DVD box sets that taught me the basics). This year it's going to be creative writing (I'll do a class or join a group) and digital art (using my iPad and Apple pencil).

I figure I can play around with my copious interests over time. But trying too many at once takes the pleasure out of it.

Personal Style

Like many women (people?) I used to feel frazzled by the multitude of options assaulting me from my closet each day. How to assemble an outfit from that confused mess?

Some people thrive on choice. I get immobilized by it.

A sense of wardrobe overwhelm is what led me to my 3-color closet minimalist approach to personal style (see *How To Curate An Introvert-Friendly Closet*). Working out my three core colors, radically decluttering everything else, and letting future purchases be guided by this limited palette. Buying more expensive pieces, but far fewer, and spending less overall.

This simplified system of closet taming has made it a breeze to shop, a pleasure to survey my wardrobe, and a surprising amount of fun to get dressed.

Dining Loyalty

Where I live is surrounded by takeaway options. Neither Craig nor I cook, so this is fabulously convenient and also a good way to avoid burning down the apartment or poisoning ourselves.

We could dine somewhere different every night of the month, but we tend to keep going back to the same few places. This might sound terribly boring to some, but I love it. For a few reasons.

For one, I seem to be pathologically incapable of ordering a standard menu item, which leads to a complicated ordering procedure everywhere I go. (I'm pretty sure my menu adjustments are vast improvements, so …)

Anyway, once they know me and my order, even if I forget one of my tweaks, they always remind me. I also get preferential treatment, free stuff, and my order often gets expedited when there's a crowd. Plus there's always a pleasant exchange, warm smiles, a nice little bit of human interaction. And I feel as though my food is made with love. Probably that's dumb but it's how it feels. I like that the people who cooked for me, like me.

There's a place near me that treats every customer as a minor nuisance. Everything is a problem. *You mean you want to pay by* credit card? *You want to order right now, over the phone??* They seem perpetually irritated that people keep turning up to give them money for food. I went there a few times when I first moved nearby, but after a while I realized it was always an unpleasant experience, and I stopped.

I feel good being loyal to the places that look after me and have a little love in their hearts. It makes dining decisions easier and it makes me happier.

Fitness

My entire fitness regime consists of one thing — body combat classes. This works for me largely because, despite the pretension to martial arts, it is essentially dancing. Choreographed moves to music. I dance around and sing loudly and off-key and fitness occurs and muscles develop completely as a by-product.

People often ask me if after all my years of combat classes I could defend myself against an assailant. The answer is *yes, definitely*. Of course I would have to ask them to wait while I found and cued the right music on my phone, and they'd have to stand in the right spot so I could aim my kicks, and they'd possibly run away quickly once I started singing. But yeah, I could take 'em.

Perhaps a minimalist fitness program is a personality thing. My extroverted friends prefer variety and wonder how I don't get bored.

Although doing one thing must deprive me of the benefits of a broader, more balanced fitness program, what I gain is the opportunity to really focus on technique and improvement. Wanting to get better, even at a strange, pugilistic form of dancing, is tremendously motivating. It keeps me turning up to the gym, day after day, week after week, pizza after pizza.

*

Not everyone is a multi-tasker who thrives on having multiple balls in the air. Don't worry what others do. Don't feel there's something wrong with you.

Maybe you're a minimalist introvert like me, who is easily overwhelmed but finds strength in simplicity. If so, then going deep rather than broad might be a very happy, effective, and peaceful way for you to live.

How To Be A Kind Introvert (Hint: Stop Being So Damned Nice)

The other day I was crossing a busy street at a walk sign. An old couple was also crossing, s-l-o-w-l-y. As I began to overtake them I noticed a car edging close, trying to intimidate them into speeding up. I slowed and moved between the couple and the car, pacing myself with the couple and making eye contact — not aggressive, but deliberate — with the driver. The car stopped pushing closer, clearly cowed by my 160cm frame and combat-honed muscles. The elderly lady whispered *Oh thank you dear, you're so kind,* as she and the man continued their protracted progress. We got to the other side and I wished the couple a happy day and walked on.

But the truth is, my small good deed was instinctive and took neither thought nor effort, so it deserved no credit. It was a basic, fellow-human thing, probably programmed into my DNA because, evolutionarily speaking, it has social value.

But— not so fast! Being kind to strangers is not always so easy. Especially if you're an introvert.

Especially if you preemptively dislike strangers because it simply saves time. Especially if you often feel all peopled out. How was it that an extreme introvert like me could act out of character — approaching strangers, making eye contact in a potentially threatening situation? And do it easily, comfortably, happily?

This wasn't even an isolated thing. I've often encouraged new, struggling participants in combat class, spoken to strangers who seemed to be in distress, offered help to random individuals. Yes friends, I'm talking about proactive, voluntary interactions with unknown persons. *Egads!*

I believe the reason I can easily be kind is that I don't deplete my people battery by being nice.

Your people battery? you sigh with resignation. *Another one of your theories?*

Yes, my *people battery*. Let me explain.

My Theory of People Batteries

1. Introverts have a smaller people battery than Extroverts

The first prong of my theory is that everyone has a people battery — a store of energy for interacting with people.

The more extroverted you are, the bigger your people battery. You can chat and network and meet strangers and go to parties and toss your people resources around like mason jars at a hipster cafe and still have plenty of charge on your people battery.

Conversely, the more introverted you are, the smaller your people battery. You simply don't have a large cache of psychological resources for groups and stranger interactions and personal space invasions. You need to preserve your battery charge with care or you get all peopled out.

2. Being kind uses little battery power, being nice uses lots

The second prong of my theory is that different kinds of people interactions require different amounts of battery power.

Being kind uses little battery power. It's paltry, chicken feed — literally "food for poultry"*, which is the Latin root of paltry. (*Not even slightly the Latin root of paltry.)

This is why it was easy to help the elderly pedestrians, even for an extreme introvert like me. Being kind feels good. Psychologically, it costs nothing.

According to this theory, it's only difficult for an introvert to be kind if their people battery is flat. And you know what drains an introvert's battery faster than a bloated iOS update?

Being nice.

Being nice uses tons of battery power. It's a massive drain on an introvert's social resources.

Why is niceness so draining for an Introvert?

Being nice can involve multiple forms of social exertion and what feels to an introvert like insincerity. This can cause the average introvert to long for a zombie apocalypse and/or Armageddon in order to escape the situation.

You have to think up things to say — often phony things, not how you genuinely want to interact at all. Perhaps you have to shake hands — eww. Often you feel pressured to show interest in something that makes your eyeballs want to roll back into your head. Maybe you're asked questions that seem intrusive coming from someone you barely know. Frequently there's small talk, chit chat, superficial banter with people straight from Circle 2 of Introvert Hell. And then of course you need a fake smile plastered across your face to disguise the fact that you're *internally screaming*.

For an introvert all of this is mentally taxing and emotionally exhausting and utterly battery depleting.

Being nice versus being kind

If your default position is to always be nice, then you may wonder if there's much difference. Doesn't being kind *include* being nice?

Nuh-uh. Here are some ways **kind** and **nice** differ:

- Being nice *takes* energy, tons of it. Being kind *gives* energy — you feel enlivened by it.
- Being nice makes at best a *small* difference to someone's day. Being kind can make a *huge* difference to someone's day.
- Being nice can feel *fake*. Being kind always feels *genuine*.
- Being nice may be *superficial*. Being kind goes *deep*.

Perhaps most importantly:

- Being nice is about *you*, wanting the other person to like you. Being kind is about *them*, attending to a genuine human need.

Sweetness and vexation

I was working at home one day when there was a knock at my apartment door. No one had buzzed the building intercom, probably because I keep it turned off. *The knock was coming from inside the building.*

Irritated at losing my hard-won focus and worried about a deadline, I grumped off to answer the door. A woman I didn't know, without introducing herself or asking if it was a convenient time, hit me with a barrage of questions about the building. I blinked and heard myself interrupt, *Who are you?*

Turns out she was a prospective purchaser of one of the other apartments. I didn't know the answers to her questions and politely suggested she ask the agent. She wanted to keep talking but I said I was in the middle of something and needed to return to work.

Was I rude? Maybe. I certainly wasn't "nice".

Nice would have been faking interest in her questions, guessing at answers I had no idea about, standing there and chatting until she wound things up, while silently fretting about my deadline.

Nice would have been insincere — all sweetness on the outside and vexation on the inside.

Nice would have been getting back to work twenty minutes later having lost my train of thought and peace of mind while contributing zero help to the woman.

I'm okay with not being nice.

I don't shake hands, or show concern I don't feel over strangers' woes, or feign interest in small talk, or try to be liked by people I don't know. It's clear to me I have a Nano people battery, a minuscule quantity of resources for dealing with people, especially strangers.

I save my people juice for those I truly care about, and I always have plenty to spare for kindness.

If you run out of People Battery then stop being so damned nice

If your people battery is large enough for you to be nice and also kind, then great — do both.

But if you're always running out of people juice then consider cutting back on the things you do and say out of social niceness.

You don't have to be rude, you can remain polite and considerate. But once you feel insincerity and frustration taking over, it could be a sign you're tipping into nice territory and draining your people battery.

As an introvert you need to be protective of your people resources. It will give you heaps more energy for your loved ones. And for being kind.

How To Give Up The 4 Classic Introvert "Shoulds"

Do you sometimes feel overwhelmed by the expectations of others and the pressure of their demands? To go out, to talk more, to be something you're not? Do you fantasize about escaping, sometimes even from your precious loved ones? Do you feel guilty about these fantasies?

There's no need to get stuck in this *overwhelm-fantasy-guilt* cycle. You can save your fantasies for more constructive scenarios involving Hemsworth brothers or whatever you're into. You can use your guilt energy to start a creative project or possibly supply a small nation with an alternative fuel source.

How?

Just get rid of certain toxic *shoulds* from your life. Such *shoulds* are insidious critters, psychological termites that infect your mind and destroy the foundations of your life. You might not know they're there, but leave them unchecked and they can eat away at your happiness and peace of mind.

Instead, eradicate these *shoulds* and you'll enjoy deeper self-acceptance and more relaxation and greater energy for your, um, fantasies.

So here are the tyrannical *shoulds*. It's time to exterminate them.

4 Shoulds to Give Up If You're an Introvert

1. *I should socialize more*

You know the *exact precise perfect right* amount you should socialize? The amount that feels right for you.

For me, this is once or maybe twice a week. If there's a week when I choose to do more because there's someone I really want to see or an event I really want to attend, then I'll plan another week when I don't socialize at all.

Take into account what you do during the week. If much of your week is people-y then you may need less social time than someone whose work is solitary. It's about balance.

The thing is, you must be *honest* with yourself about what feels right. If you've fallen into a rut of never going out and it's getting you down, then push yourself to make plans. Distinguish between what genuinely feels healthy and what feels like a habit that's not serving you.

Experiment with going out a bit more or less. Within a few weeks you'll know what your ideal frequency is. Make that your weekly template and organize your social life around it.

2. I should be more spontaneous

It seems to me there are two kinds of people. Those who complete their thoughts.

Seriously though, there are those who like to be spontaneous and those who like to plan in advance. If you're like many easily overstimulated introverts, you may prefer scheduling over spontaneity, you may feel thrown by last-minute changes. That's your preference and it's a perfectly fine preference to have.

Sure, sometimes things will change without warning, and it's a mark of maturity to adapt when you have to. But the rest of the time, don't feel you have to be spontaneous if it's not what feels good to you.

Become fine with saying, *I get pleasure from planning in advance*, or *I like to enjoy anticipation,* or *I know you like surprises but I like feeling prepared.*

Or make a joke, which is a great way to express yourself without tension: *Personally I love spontaneity, as long as it's well planned and involves snacks.* It's hard to argue with this because who doesn't love snacks?

3. I should smile more

I know from the Louder Minds Facebook Group that many introverts suffer the debilitating affliction known as "Resting Bitch Face". Perhaps you've quickly looked away from someone cursed with this cruel scourge. Maybe you've thought of starting an ice bucket challenge to raise awareness.

Interestingly, introverts are less tuned-in to people's faces than are extroverts. We're probably too busy having convoluted conversations in our own heads.

For many introverts a smile is the facial equivalent of a giant "Welcome" sign, when we'd prefer a sign that says "No one's home, keep walking, buddy".

All of which makes it understandable that we are not, as a rule, big smilers. And not being a smiler is fine. Give up thinking you *should* smile more if that doesn't feel genuine to you.

As for others telling you you should smile more, try responding with something like, *But I smiled yesterday,* or, *You mean I'm not smiling now?* or, *It's the Botox,* or, *Yeah I lost my smile in a car accident in Reno in '05.*

A caveat here. Or perhaps a cravat would be better, as it's hard for someone to criticize your non-smile if they're distracted by a bright, colorful cravat tied just below your chin with a jaunty flourish.

I forgot what I was saying.

Oh yeah — a caveat. Consider how *you* feel about smiling. I realized a few years ago that I'd fallen into a habit of low-level scowling. I would go about my day with a kind of irritated glower smeared across my face. I noticed people thought I was angry — the receptionist at the gym, a salesperson at a store — and it complicated my interactions. Over time I worked at having a softer facial expression and I found I got along better with everyone I came into contact with. I can honestly say I now get great service pretty much everywhere I go, and I think part of that is having a pleasant, non-evil-glare look on my face.

So forget what you *should* do — decide what you want to do. Be genuine, be natural. But also be sure you're not unintentionally coming across as a cantankerous cranky-pants.

4. I should explain myself

If you like going out and you have a social personality and you enjoy noise and lights and heaps of things going on, then nobody is going to take you aside and ask you if you're okay.

But if you're quiet and you enjoy solitude and you're easily tired by groups and often overwhelmed and you like observing from the sidelines, then there's a good chance you will find yourself being challenged about your choices. Which can lead you to think you should explain.

But here's the lovely truth: you simply don't have to explain anything to anybody.

You'll likely want to have some honest con-versations about introversion with the people you care about, so they understand you, and your relationships can grow deeper. You may also choose to share some things about being an introvert, maybe with humor, to make your own life easier.

But as for the rest of the world, it's perfectly okay to live your life your way and have others not get it. Even to take a perverse pleasure in being somewhat inscrutable.

You can spend your energy endlessly defending yourself to people whose opinions aren't important to you, or you can spend your energy enjoying your solitary hobbies, your deep friendships, your intere-sting thoughts, your growing self-acceptance.

Which feels better to you?

*

So what do you think?

Are you going to let these *shoulds* keep burrowing into your psyche? Are you going to let others' expectations tell you how you should feel? How you should be? Or are you going to give up those *shoulds* and listen to what's right for you?

The choice is yours.

But remember — those Hemsworths are waiting.

How To Stop Procrastinating Like An Introvert

If you're an introvert then your methods of procrastination will likely differ from those of your extroverted friends.

To put off starting, an extrovert may make a phone call and chat, while an introvert might turn a simple task into an over-analyzed, over-planned, over-engineered nightmare. To dodge work, an extrovert might organize a lunch, while an introvert might organize their desk and bookshelf for the twenty-seventh time.

And if you're a creative introvert, or one who works on your own stuff from home, then you face a whole other level of challenge in order to get down to work each day.

For a decade I've been writing in my home office, surrounded by books I'd like to read and TV shows I'd like to watch and countless other not-work things I'd like to do. So I've learned a thing or two about procrastination. Over the years these insights have shaped the way I work and boosted both my productivity and the pleasure I get from my work. I think they'll help you, too.

4 Insights about Procrastination that have changed the way I work

Insight #1: Wanting to procrastinate is not the problem

Let's get one thing clear: starting is hard. And if starting involves being in your own head with its perfectionism and self-doubt and rampant over-thinking, if it involves facing the existential abyss that is a blank page, then it's incredibly hard.

Wanting to avoid starting is not only natural, it's smart. If you always went willingly to a difficult fate then one might question the quality of your cognitive functioning.

No, procrastination is not your enemy — *and realizing this is liberating*. It stops you resisting feelings of avoidance, which are normal. It stops you beating yourself up for laziness or a weak character, which you don't have. It stops you doing battle with procrastination, which is not the issue, and lets you focus on what is:

The inescapable reality that starting is just plain hard.

Blaming your urge to procrastinate for not starting is like blaming your desire to eat donuts for eating too many donuts. *Of course* you want to eat donuts — they taste good. Wanting to eat something that tastes good and wanting to avoid something that's hard is human nature.

Donuts taste good, starting is hard. Get to the root of the issue.

Resisting procrastination is actually an excellent *way* to procrastinate. You can google solutions. You can lie on your couch and psychoanalyze yourself while stroking your beard. You can trace it all back to that childhood trauma when someone replaced your choc-chip muffin with a gluten-free kale sandwich.

All of which stops you from getting your butt in your chair and simply … starting.

Don't waste your time and energy fighting procrastination. Procrastination is nothing more complicated than your mind saying that doing what matters to you is difficult.

Thank you, mind, you are right.

It *is* difficult. Starting is hard.

Insight #2: Pulling works better than pushing

This is not a digression into the esoteric art of knot tying.

I've experimented with many ways to motivate myself over the years. When I've tried to *make* myself go sit at my desk and do my work, it's always been a fight. But when I've felt *drawn* to that same work, when it's *enticed* me, then much of the fight has simply disappeared.

A lot of this comes down to *why* you're doing something. If it's coming from a place of *should* then yeah, you are stuck in push territory. This is like taking up running because the doctor says you ought to lose weight after you broke his scales that time. It was one time!

Compare this to coming from a place of *want*. Taking up running because you want to feel fitter and stronger and enjoy the thrill of a marathon.

(Um, *the thrill of a marathon*? Who is coming up with these examples? What was wrong with the donuts?)

Another thing that can turn a push into a pull is time. Sometimes I resist work because it's not fully baked, the idea needs to incubate further. Sometimes your mind knows you're not ready and is stalling for time.

For me, these are excellent opportunities to go do a combat class, or work on something that uses my brain in a different way. This is a strategy I call "proconstructinating".

Insight #3: "Proconstructinating" is a valuable strategy

So what is proconstructinating? It's procrastinating constructively — avoiding what you "should" be doing but still achieving something useful.

Sometimes I want to avoid the precise thing I know I should be doing. It's a kind of childishness, or rebelliousness, or maybe it's just human nature. Whatever causes it, it makes me feel that I really *really* don't want to do the *right* thing.

A while ago I realized I could make this work for me if I set up my work in a cunning way. So here's what I do. I make sure I always have a range of tasks to work on, usually a nicely written list on pretty notepaper. I survey my list and identify the task that's most important. Almost instantly I develop a strange longing to do *anything* else, so I happily throw myself into one of those other tasks just to escape the main one.

Ha ha, I chuckle to myself, gleefully dodging item #1 on my to-do list while conscientiously making my way through items #2 to #7.

Now if you think this sounds like I'm dealing with a child, then, well, what's your point? Perhaps you're more grown-up than I am; in fact, you almost certainly are. Still, if you struggle with procrastination then I suspect you, too, have an obstinate little child in you who can be effectively wrangled with strategies not unlike those of a Supernanny.

Once you accept that you have an inner child who doesn't want to be told what to do, you can provide options that allow you to rebel and *still* make progress.

I also like to think of this as surfing the motivation wave — giving myself permission to work on whatever I feel like each day, as much as possible. Taking the *should* out of my work, the pressure, the push, helps me "give in" to procrastination while still being quite prodigiously productive.

And you know what? The cool thing is that once I start making progress, the important task I've been avoiding doesn't feel so onerous, and I often find myself slipping into it without further evasions or tantrums, and only the whispered promise of a chocolate bar.

Insight 4: In the end you have to be like ABBA

By "be like ABBA" I don't mean you should grab a hairbrush and belt out "Super Trouper". Though I'm not going to lie to you, typing the name of that song did make me do just that.

But no, I have something else in mind.

I've gone through phases when I'd wait for inspiration to hit before going to my desk. This is also known variously as *kidding yourself; achieving nothing;* and *yeah how's that working out for ya?*

At times when I think my talent is so rarefied that I must wait for the muse to stir imagination to life, I remind myself of an interview I read years ago with the members of ABBA. Björn Ulvaeus and Benny Andersson, the songwriters, would have breakfast every morning and then go outside to their studio. There, guitar in hand, butt on piano stool, they would work and work and work. Composing music. Writing lyrics (not even in their first language). Creating harmonies.

Muse or no muse. Inspiration or no inspiration. Rain, hail, or snow. Though often snow, because after all they lived in Sweden.

They were creative geniuses. Love or hate* their music (*I'm sorry, we can't be friends anymore), it would be hard to find another body of work as large where each song is so singular — I can't think of two ABBA songs that have similar melodies.

You'd think such outstanding creativity would be the product of wild inspiration. Or drug-fueled invention. But no. It was simply:

1. Being in the place where the work is done and
2. Doing the work.

There really is nothing else.

Change how you think about Procrastination

Don't let procrastination become a monster with which you do battle, sapping your energy, wasting your time. Procrastination is not the problem!

The problem is that starting is hard.

You can make it easier to start if you *acknowledge* that starting is genuinely difficult.

You can make it easier to start if you remind yourself *why* you want to do this.

You can make it easier to start if you let yourself start *anywhere*, wherever you feel like.

You make it easier to start if you're *sitting on your chair*, at your desk, with your fingers on the keys.

In fact, maybe you can go start right now.

How The Show *Friends* Can Make You A Happier Introvert

One of my all-time favorite TV comedies is *Friends*. I've watched every episode at least twice, yeah, okay four times. Joey and Chandler's friendship is in my top five screen relationships ever. And I still find the 'camera' bit, when the gang is watching an old video of Monica, hilarious. (Joey: *Some girl ate Monica!* Monica: *Shut up, the camera adds ten pounds.* Chandler: *Ah, so how many cameras are actually on you?*)

But *Friends* has also been a huge source of angst for me.

I first watched it before I knew about introversion, or that I myself was at the extreme end of the introvert spectrum. I would see these people hanging out all the time and yearn for that kind of friendship. I was 40 percent Monica (neat freak), 40 percent Chandler (sarcastic quipper) and 20 percent Ross (judgmental nerd), so I figured I was destined to be part of a similarly hilarious sextet.

Yet when I had the opportunity to spend time with my own friends, I often avoided it, preferring to stay home and be neat and quippy and nerdy all by myself. It made no sense, and it left me confused, frustrated, and unhappy.

I understand now that the group of friends I craved was not only *like* the characters in *Friends*, it *was* the characters in *Friends*. Hanging out with them let me *be* with people without being with *actual* people. Which can be very comforting for an introvert.

But I also understand now that *Friends* was one of many places I saw extroverts as the norm, which led me to feel there was something intrinsically wrong with me.

The Ideal, Extroverted Self

In many ways, we are introverts living in an extrovert world. That sentence may evoke Madonna in your head, or perhaps The Police. Both are great choices but they do show your age. Personally I'm too young to get the references.

The point is, as introverts, who we are is often at odds with the model of successful, happy people we see in the world around us.

In TV and movies extroverted characters dominate — and it makes sense. Stories about introverts wouldn't have the same narrative drive —

also known as "anything visible happening" — as stories about extroverts, with their adventures and their social lives and their conversations that take place *outside* their heads.

In social and old media too, extroverts are the ones we see making movies, gyrating in music videos, posing in selfies, giving interviews, being visible. Being audible.

Quiet author Susan Cain says, "In our society, the ideal self is bold, gregarious, and comfortable in the spotlight. We … admire the type of individual who's comfortable 'putting himself out there.' Our schools, workplaces, and religious institutions are designed for extroverts."

By definition the "ideal self" that is visible to us is the one "putting himself out there", comfortable in the spotlight.

Although there are many hugely successful introverts — from Albert Einstein to Bill Gates to Dr. Seuss — they may be harder to see because the only spotlight they're totally comfortable in is probably a really good reading lamp.

Being a Happy Introvert

The important thing, and one of the key messages of this book, is that introverts and extroverts each find happiness in different ways.

We each need to do what feels right for us. Or perhaps more precisely, we need to do what stops us from feeling miserable and uncomfortable. For the extrovert, too *little* stimulation may feel like depression; for the introvert, too *much* might feel like anxiety.

Research shows extroverts are more sensation-seeking, more tuned in to faces, and more inclined to wear eye-catching outfits, which means their more social, more out-there, more adventurous choices make sense.

So, as introverts, we need to not judge extroverts for their choices, *nor ourselves for ours*. We need to nurture our own self-acceptance and enjoy happiness in our own way. We need to be mindful that the "ideal self" dominating much of TV, movies, and social media is not *our* ideal self.

Because how many cameras are on introverts like us? Usually, none.

How To Help Extroverts Understand You Better

(To the owner of this book: Here's something you can leave carelessly open and lying around for your extroverted partner, friend, boss or colleague to find.)

Dear Extrovert

Pssst, lovely extrovert! Here are seven pieces of information about introverts that will make your life easier, your relationship better, and your hair shinier.

Note: As we've discussed in earlier chapters, there are no pure introverts or extroverts, rather, there's an introvert-extrovert spectrum on which people fall. I'm using the terms introvert and extrovert to refer to people who fall toward one extreme more than the other.

1. Introverts and Extroverts are wired differently

Maybe you think being an introvert is a bit like being a hipster — a fad, and to be honest, kind of annoying.

Your introvert won't go out when you want, or talk as much as you'd like, or be as adventurous. You wish they'd come out of their shell. At least long enough to try skydiving. Or even just answer their phone for goodness sake.

In fact scientific research shows the difference between introverts and extroverts is biologically based, right down to the amount of gray matter in our brains. Where a person falls on the introvert-extrovert spectrum is one of five fundamental aspects of who we are.

So your introvert's introversion is not some bogus classification like their star sign or BMI. It's an intrinsic, scientific, neurological part of them.

2. Introverts and Extroverts have the same drive, but in different directions

Although introverts and extroverts differ in many ways, the difference at the heart of many relationship issues is one of stimulation and arousal. Uh no, this is a *different* issue of stimulation and arousal. If you've lost interest now, no hard feelings. Um, moving on.

Extroverts have a lower baseline level of arousal than introverts. They need to turn up the stimulation dial otherwise they can feel depressed, bored, and uncomfortable. This is why they seek out adventure, challenge, and socializing. Why they like noise and lights and multiple things going on and lots of balls in the air. Why they crave them.

In contrast, introverts have a higher baseline level of arousal. They need to turn down the stimulation dial or they can feel stressed, anxious, and uncomfortable. This is why they seek out solitude and internal activities like reading and mental work. Why they can't handle too much going on.

The same drive to feel comfortable in your own skin compels both introverts and extroverts. It simply drives introverts and extroverts in different directions.

3. Introverts don't need to be fixed

If you've been trying to convince your introvert to come out of their shell, be more adventurous, or socialize more, then you're probably picking little bits of brick out of your forehead about now.

You're coming from a place of love: *you* feel happy when you do these things, and you want your introvert to be happy too. Plus we tend to conceptualize a happy person as gregarious, out-there, social.

But the thing is, introverts *enjoy* solitude. They *like* their own company. They're *happy* observing rather than participating. They don't need to be rescued or fixed or changed any more than a gregarious, always-busy, adventurous extrovert does.

They're not depressed, they're not miserable, they're just lower key. And they want to be happy in their own way. So let them.

Note: Of course you can have a depressed introvert, but that's a whole other thing and beyond the scope of this book.

4. It's not personal when an Introvert wants Alone Time

Because introverts have a higher baseline level of arousal they can easily become overstimulated and feel overwhelmed — a state I call "introvert overload".

This is entirely to do with depleted psychological resources. It's like a battery that runs out of juice and needs to pop out of the remote and slot into a battery charger and refuel. The battery is not mad at anyone. It hasn't lost interest in the remote. It doesn't hate all electronic devices. Just let it quietly recharge and it will be back powering your binge-viewing in no time.

I know it can *feel* personal when someone says they need time and space. But if they tell you it's because they're suffering introvert overload and they just need to reset their psychological systems to normal, take a chance they're telling the truth and see what happens. They will probably love you more for it.

5. We all have a "Socializing versus Solitude" sweet spot

A good way to think about the socializing difference between introverts and extroverts is the concept of equilibrium. We all have a level of "socializing versus solitude" that feels good. The baby-bear spot. The sweet spot where we feel neither under-stimulated/depressed/bored, nor overstimulated/stressed/anxious, but *just right*. And we all feel happier when we hover around our personal level of equilibrium.

The more extroverted you are, the more likely this level will be found in a mix that has plenty of activity, sociability, adventure, and spontaneity.

The more introverted you are, the more likely your equilibrium level will involve plenty of solitude, quiet activities, and solo pastimes.

Wherever you fall on the introvert-extrovert spectrum, accepting yourself for the way you are helps you make decisions that keep you in your sweet spot. And this self-acceptance makes you more willing to accept other people for the way they are too — whether introvert, extrovert, ambivert, or whatever. Which means more happiness and acceptance for everybody.

6. Introverts don't hate people

To a non-introvert, the introvert's resistance to socializing and joining in can seem like misanthropy.

Why do you hate people? you want to ask. *How did your heart get so cold?* you whisper to yourself, your voice trembling from the emotion of it all.

It's closer to the truth to say that introverts feel *too much*.

Introverts have a higher baseline level of arousal than extroverts, remember. Plus they literally use up more mental resources scanning and processing external stimuli. Which means being with people can take a pretty big psychological toll.

So it's not that introverts don't *like* people, it's that they find the experience of being with people very intense — not unlike the feeling of too much noise and light. This sense of overstimulation pushes them into the red zone where the psychological sirens start to scream. Considering this, it makes sense that introverts save their people time for the people who really matter.

Which leads me to …

7. You mean a great deal to your Introvert

If an introvert has sent you to this book, it's because you mean a great deal to them.

Because introverts get easily peopled-out, they tend to focus their energies on the relationships that matter most. They can be reserved or even aloof with the vast majority of people. It's just easier than trying to explain.

But if they've sent you here, then they *want* you to understand. You matter to your introvert.

If you take just one thing from this chapter then, remember that the same drive that compels extroverts to want to be *with people* compels introverts to want to be *alone*. You matter to them — they're simply wired differently, and they show they care in another way.

And their way of showing they care may be asking you to read this, so you can understand each other better. Thank you for doing that! I hope these seven insights about introverts have shed some light on the topic. Not *too* much light though …

*

So what now?

Well, if this all makes sense, then let the introvert in your life know. Go drop in on them spontaneously. Suggest a huge impromptu slumber party. Or call them up and have a good old long chin-wag.

Good luck with that!

How To Switch Off And
Sleep Better

If I were a fairytale princess, you know which one
I'd be?

Not Sleeping Beauty, that's for sure. Seriously,
what drugs is she on to sleep like that? Also, um, do
you know where she gets them?

Possibly Cinderella, as I always like to leave
parties before midnight. Plus I like cute heels and am
just absent-minded enough to lose one. But I lack
domestic skills, and as a rule prefer to dress without
avian assistance — so maybe not.

No, if I were a fairytale princess I'd be the one in
The Princess And The Pea. The one who had multiple
mattresses and still couldn't sleep. *Because there was
a pea in the bed*. She sounds just like me.

The Introverted Princess and the Pea

Honestly, is this not a great metaphor for what it's
like to be an introvert? Noticing *every little thing*?

Being hypersensitive? And, let's be honest, getting uppity over what seems like *nothing* to others?

But for those of us who aren't great sleepers, the resonance of this fairytale is not merely metaphorical.

My bed has to be well made. The sheets must be pulled tight. I like to have my eye-mask and earplugs. A glass of water by the bed and a towering reading pile to lull myself to sleepiness. Things have to be pea-free.

My husband is one of those easy sleepers. We both read in bed, but when he's ready, he simply turns out his bedside lamp, closes his eyes, and (I kid you not) *falls asleep*.

On the rare occasions he doesn't immediately drift off, the conversation goes like this:

Craig: "I'm not sleepy!"

Me (finishing the paragraph I'm reading): "You'll be asleep in no time."

Craig (annoyed): "What? You woke me up."

I'm not even exaggerating.

But although I'm not going to win any prizes for sleeping (a Snoozy?), I have managed to improve my sleep quality over time.

One thing that made a huge difference was having surgery on my nose a couple of years ago. Before that I would wake myself throughout the night with wheezing, whistling, and various other nasal orchestrations. Honestly, it was like a Philip Glass opera in there.

But once that was solved, it became clear I was still a poor sleeper and needed to look further for solutions.

So I stopped drinking caffeine after midday. That was a very difficult time and I don't like to think about the many people who suffered during the adjustment.

More recently I experimented with a 15-minute mindfulness practice every day. Me and mindfulness are like chalk and cheese — only one goes well with a lovely Shiraz. (I probably should have worked harder on that simile but I get distracted when cheese is involved.) It was not a success.

Still, I would lie awake for ages, my brain abuzz. Mentally drafting blog posts in my head. Making to-do lists, thoroughly categorized and color-coded. Trying to visualize Gantt charts. Ruminating. Getting anxious about my anxiety.

Eventually I realized what was missing from my approach. No, not a good swig of a single malt, though I considered it. Okay, yeah, there may have been some occasional late-night swilling.

What I needed was a longer period to disengage from the thinking and working part of my day.

Are you a Quick Switcher or a Slow Switcher?

Here's what I worked out.

I'm a slow switcher. It takes me ages to warm up and get into something. But once I do, I have good momentum. Then it's actually hard for me to stop. I've found this with exercising, writing, learning French, studying — pretty much everything.

I'd much rather do any kind of endurance exercise, like a long walk or a long combat class, than suffer the start-stop of even a short interval-training session — which to me is torment in trainers. If I were ever captured and asked to reveal secrets (of which I thankfully know none), I'd only have to be threatened with 8-seconds on/8-seconds off on the treadmill and I'd sing like an off-key canary.

I'd much rather batch my work tasks and have entire days each for writing, research, and admin, than do a little of everything every day. On "everything days" I feel like I waste half the time getting into each new task.

So here's my theory: Because of my slowness to switch, when my mind is in work mode it stays overactive for some time before letting go. Like an electric oven versus a gas one, I guess. (I don't cook so I'm hoping this analogy works.)

Before I cottoned on to this switching idea, I would often do an online check-in right before bed — email, Facebook page, blog, Facebook group.

Now here's where this was seductive. If there was nothing that needed my attention, I'd feel all happy and peaceful as I went to bed. So that made it *positively* reinforcing. It was lovely to do that late-night check-in and know that all was well. I was actually just checking in to get this reassurance.

But seeking reassurance is always a double-edged sword.

What if all is not serene? What if someone has asked a question that you feel you should respond to? What if there's an email that gets you (over)thinking?

Often I would see something that could easily wait till morning, but once I'd seen it, it bothered and distracted me until I dealt with it. I'd have to answer the email. Reply to the comment. Return the message. Some people can put these things aside — that's never been easy for me.

You guys, this niggling little thing is a pea. A nothing. But one that can keep you up for ages.

So what would happen? I'd go to my desk and deal with the pea and get dragged back into work mode and my brain would get provoked and I'd need to disengage all over again.

So what do I do now? I now have a discrete shut-down ritual. (Thanks to Cal Newport's book *Deep Work* for the idea of designing a shut-down ritual.)

My Shut-Down/Switch-Off Ritual

1. When I'm done with work for the day, I tick off the to-do items I've completed (I love this part!)

and transfer any incomplete items to the days I plan to work on them.

2. I leave my browser tabs open (you'll see why) and take a shower. I generally play music and I find that really helps me unwind. I may or may not grab a shampoo bottle and sing along.

3. Invariably I have a bunch of ideas in the shower.

4. After my shower I add any ideas that have survived the vocal extravaganza to my diary or I create drafts in my still-open blog browser tab.

5. I do a final check of email and social media.

6. Then — this is the most important part — I close my browser tabs, plug in my phone to charge, turn off my monitor, close my diary, and turn off my office lamp. This little ritual makes me feel like I'm pulling up the drawbridge on work and letting my brain move into relaxation phase. It's really therapeutic!

7. Next I watch some TV. Often an episode of a European crime show, or some stand-up comedy.

8. In bed I read until I feel sleepy, then try to put down my book, turn out my lamp, and snuggle down to sleep before my brain knows what's going on and has a chance to get all fidgety about something that can totally wait till tomorrow.

Adding this shut-down ritual to my life has been great. I'm less distracted while watching my TV shows and while reading, so I enjoy them both more.

I sleep better. And whatever is waiting for me online is still there in the morning.

I doubt I'll ever sleep as soundly as Sleeping Beauty. I have my doubts about her.

But those peas? I am getting better at knowing they'll be there in the morning. And not taking them into bed with me at night.

How To Curate An Introvert-Friendly Closet

Simplicity is the keynote of all true elegance.

Coco Chanel

Did you know that, compared to introverts, extroverts wear more eye-catching outfits? I imagine part of the reason is that introverts ~~like to hide~~ don't like to draw attention to themselves.

But I also think introverts find simplicity and minimalism more peaceful and beautiful. A simple wardrobe is visually calming and less likely to over-stimulate. Plus it makes outfit decision-making simpler, so it's less likely to overwhelm.

I used to stand in front of my closet, paralyzed by choice, feeling defeated by the pressure to pull together an outfit from so many possibilities. My overflowing closet, rather than offering lots of great options, was simply a source of stress. And it often made me late, a trail of discarded clothes in my wake as I rushed, frazzled, out the door to wherever I was going. So much for calm self-possession.

But then I discovered a way to simplify my life, and ease the pressure on my sad little overwhelmed brain, and also make my closet look more aesthetically pleasing. Here's what I did.

My 3CC: 3-Color Closet

Over some months, I reduced my closet to mainly 3 colors.

I chose 3 neutral colors I could mix and match

I chose: black, navy, and white.

I could wear black + white, navy + white, black + navy (a favorite combination of mine — but if it's not your taste, choose something else), all black, or all navy.

I created a theme

I already had some good basics in these colors and I bought several more. That gave me a solid base of boots, heels, coats, jackets, jeans, tops, sweaters, skirts, and handbags.

And, knowing I'd be wearing these staples for years, I bought classic designs, not trendy ones, and I bought the best quality I could afford.

This was my *theme*.

I added variation

For variety and a touch of personality, I bought the odd accent item, or more trend-based pieces like inexpensive tops and jeans, in colors like pink and blue.

And I was happy to pay less and not worry so much about quality, as I knew I'd just wear them for a season or two, as a highlight.

This was my *variation*.

With numerous colors removed, basics streamlined, and accents reduced to the occasional piece, I radically decreased the number of items I needed. It was genius.

Fashion changes, but style endures

Coco Chanel

Why have a 3-Color Closet?

Should you try a 3-color closet? What are the advantages of my approach?

1. The 3CC simplifies shopping and saves money

Shopping becomes far easier. For one thing, you have so much less in your closet, so it's easier to remember what you have and therefore not buy what you don't need.

Plus, you don't crave that retail high anymore. It's so pleasurable to enjoy your simple, uncluttered closet — and that makes you hold every potential purchase to a higher standard. I buy more expensive items now, but overall I spend far less since I've switched to my 3CC.

Decision-making when you shop is a cinch as well. *Doesn't come in one of my colors? Hmm I'll leave it.* Easy.

2. The 3CC simplifies dressing and assembling outfits

Because my closet is mostly in these three colors, everything literally goes with everything else. Here's my process:

- I usually pick one thing I feel like wearing. If it's a strong piece — like leather pants or over-the-knee boots — I choose something simple to go with it. If it's very plain — say classic skinny jeans in indigo — then I might opt for a top with some kind of detailing. One fancy item per outfit is my limit.
- All my jackets, coats, footwear, and handbags are in my three neutral hues, so they all go with everything. I simply make a choice based on day versus evening, weather, and formality of the occasion.

From one single decision, my outfits pretty well assemble themselves.

3. The 3CC saves time

I go shopping and wander around stores far less than I used to.

When I do shop I'm more focused and efficient because my parameters are so clear.

I spend much less time getting dressed.

I rarely spend time putting away a maelstrom of discarded clothes.

4. The 3CC looks beautiful

A closet of three neutral colors just looks lovely. Especially when the clothes are beautifully spaced instead of smooshed together in a horrible over-crowded clump.

Having matching hangers (no wires, ew) helps too.

Women think of all colors except the absence of color. I have said that black has it all. White too. Their beauty is absolute. It is the perfect harmony.

Coco Chanel

How to transition to a 3-Color Closet

If you love having a radically different look every day, then this approach is not for you. If you like your style to be about the *clothes* rather than the person, then this approach is not for you. If you like to have the latest trend in fashion, then this approach is not for you. If your idea of introvert style is a heavy goth look best described as "Back Away Slowly", then this approach is definitely not for you.

But if you find classic minimalism is more your thing, then my 3CC could be perfect for you.

Don't worry if your current closet contains more shades than a sunglasses factory. Here's how to make the transition:

1. Get rid of all your closet dross. If you haven't worn it in a year, if it doesn't fit, if it doesn't look good or feel good or make you happy — donate it or toss it out. Regardless of color! Out damn skort, to paraphrase Lady Macbeth.

2. Of your remaining items, see if there's a theme in your colors. If you already have mainly chocolate, cream, and camel; or black, white, and taupe; or coral, cream, and beige, then you can make this work beautifully. If you have an overabundance of chartreuse then I think we're both out of our depths.

3. If there's no existing color theme, then peruse fashion magazines or store windows to see what colors you like. Look for colors that work well together and appeal to you and pick your three.

4. Add to your closet over time, buying classic styles in your neutral color choices. Let this happen organically, in line with your budget and wardrobe needs.

5. Buy the odd accent item in a non-neutral color, but make this an occasional purchase only.

6. Continue to prune your closet — every time you make a new purchase, look for at least one thing to donate. Keep moving toward those classic pieces in your signature colors, with a few fun accents each season.

Over time you'll create a wardrobe of classic, neutral pieces that all go together, are a pleasure to wear, and look lovely in your closet.

Now comes the true introvert challenge: *making plans* so you can get dressed and actually leave the house in your simple but beautiful outfit!

How To Find Your Introvert Happy Places

The world is full of noise, crowds, and rambunctious people. Bars, open-plan offices, crowded trains and buses, busy city streets — all these can leave us feeling trapped and suffocated, uncomfortable and all peopled-out.

But the world also offers places where a more reflective soul can find peace, contentment, solace, or even the right kind of company. Here are five places an introvert can enjoy a calmer kind of happy.

1. The Cafe Office

Many introverts like being or working alone, but *with other people.* A coffee shop is a great place to do this — whether it's to enjoy the hubbub of humanity without having to engage, or to people-watch.

I like to write at cafes a couple of days a week. I found a place that made great coffee, but it was right in the middle of a shopping center and acquaintances kept finding me and stopping to chat. Eeek!

After some experimentation I found a cafe that's hidden away, where they've learned how I like my coffee and they make me a delicious lunch that's not even on the menu. I never have to order — they know my routine and take great care of me while I work.

If you're prepared to do a little exploring you might track down a coffee shop that offers a quiet corner and good coffee. If you do, become a regular and be a good customer. Order generously for the time you're there, and tip well.

If you work in a loud workplace perhaps you can negotiate some regular time at your own little cafe office. Find a way to demonstrate you're more productive there, and your boss will be happy.

2. The Park, Beach, or Walking Trail Escape

What could be better than taking your book, Kindle, iPad, or notebook to a picturesque spot in the park?

For me, staying inside could be better, a lot better, and also freer of bugs. But this is not about me and the heinousness of bugs with their creepy bug bodies and their weird, excessive bug legs.

If you enjoy the outdoors then find a spot on the grass or on a bench under a shady tree, and enjoy the birds and the breeze and the fresh air.

Or perhaps the background sound of crashing waves on a deserted beach is more your thing? Or a trek through a picturesque hiking trail?

Personally, my absolute favorite thing about the outdoors is coming back inside. But if you enjoy nature, investigate local spots where you can enjoy some outdoorsy-ness and quality introvert time.

3. The Sofa + TV Combo

I'm sure I don't need to sell you on the formula of *sofa + TV = introvert joy*. But for me there's a third ingredient that makes the sofa/TV combo a truly happy introvert place. No, not snacks, though of course you're right and I stand corrected. And now also hungry.

The thing that elevates quality sofa and TV time for me is when it *rewards* a period of hard work rather than provides a way to *avoid* it. When I watch TV because I'm feeling overwhelmed or want to procrastinate, there's always this little mental barrier to really enjoying myself.

But if I've done some good work and my brain is happily tired, there's a whole other level of pleasure. So I use TV as an incentive and work toward it. Right now I have a long, challenging list of tasks I'm working through and when I'm done my reward will be to binge-watch a fun new series. Of course I could start doing that now, but the pleasure will be sweeter when it feels earned.

Whether you like learning from documentaries, escaping into other worlds, or "hanging out" with people who don't need anything from you, the sofa + TV combination can be a very restorative place for introverts.

4. The Friend Dinner Date

Although many of us introverts dislike parties and large-scale social events, we may really enjoy time with our best friends.

I love to have friend dates, when I get together over dinner with a close friend. For an introvert there's something very nurturing about deep conversation with a dear friend over a delicious meal. And wine. Did I mention there should be good wine?

For this reason I always choose restaurants that have the right ambience — not too noisy, not too brightly lit, not rushed, tables not too jammed together. I usually wear something a little dressy as well — it just feels good.

If you don't have regular friend dates, give it a try. It's a lovely and rejuvenating way to spend an evening.

5. The Library

If you enjoy books and quiet and have a library near you then you are indeed a lucky introvert. This may be one of the most wonderful places for someone seeking a serene place to spend some time.

There's the smell of books, the helpful librarians, and even the officious, cranky ones (I find them strangely comforting). There's the camaraderie of fellow booklovers with whom you do not have to interact in any way, and the lovely dependability of the Dewey Decimal System. There's the "new books" section, and the fact you can stroll around and look at spines and search the catalogue and let one thing lead to another as you explore and read and explore some more.

One piece of advice though: if it's peace you're after, be sure to avoid children's story-time.

How To Stop Making Unhelpful Comparisons

I used to compare myself to others. But now I'm better than most. ☺

Perhaps as introverts we compare more, given our tendency to be more internally aroused, our tendency to make judgments.

But there are three kinds of comparisons that can be pretty toxic. Especially for introverts who are reflective and inward focused. Here are three types of comparisons you should be alert to avoid.

3 Comparisons You Should Stop Making

1. Comparing your best to their worst

This kind of comparison can be unintentional but harsh, a judgmental diatribe flying unbidden into your brain.

You might find the uppity little voice in your head coming down hard on:

- The person who says a really dumb thing
- The person whose outfit looks faintly ridiculous
- The person who's trying way too hard
- The person who walks erratically into your path while typing on their phone
- The clueless person with the pram blocking everyone's path
- The person who waits till they get off the escalator to stop and ponder where they want to go.

It's easy to rant an internal tirade at that person.

Unlike we, who (at this particular moment) are at the top of our game. Smart, considerate, good-looking — humans who are simply superior to this irritating specimen. *Model* humans, really.

But the thing is, these are silly things we've all done at one time or another. If not this exact thing then something equivalently dim-witted or inconsiderate. It's only because we're not doing it *right now* that we can feel superior to the person who is.

I'm terribly guilty of this kind of comparison. The voice in my head can be like a director's commentary, judging and condemning and huffing away without pause for breath, and making it impossible to enjoy the feature.

Yet my own showreel of idiotic things said and done would make Adam Sandler outtakes look like a Merchant Ivory film.

This mental comparison has unpleasant consequences. It can put you in a bad mood and leave you feeling (even more) misanthropic. It can set a nasty little scowl on your face. If you direct your thoughts into a passive-aggressive glare or eye roll or sigh then you can make the other person feel pretty awful too.

Much better to temper your annoyance by remembering we all do and say dumb things and assume you're just seeing this person at a bad moment. Share an understanding smile, lend a hand to help, or simply say a silent thank you that you're not the one being a doofus right now.

At worst, you keep your equanimity — a precious thing to an overanalyzing introvert. At best, you may be the bright spot in the other person's bad day. How lovely is that!

As Jean Giraudoux said, "Only the mediocre are always at their best." Assume those annoying people are simply not at their best right now.

2. Comparing your worst to their best

This kind of comparison is a special horror of Facebook and other social media.

> POST: Here I am doing something super cool.
>
> REALITY: I rarely do anything interesting so there's no way I'm not sharing this.

POST: Here I am lying in bed looking amazing without makeup.

REALITY: I took 47 shots at various angles and tried 12 filters before settling on this pic.

POST: Here I am being uber successful in my business and having the time of my life.

REALITY: It's hard to get any traction and I have to hit up all my friends.

POST: Here I am living my fabulous life in my fabulous home with my fabulous family.

REALITY: Sometimes I want to murder them all and burn the house down while drinking a box of wine.

And the people who post these statuses are themselves looking to feel better in a social media world of constant comparison.

Still, such curated snippets of supposed "real life" can leave us feeling down on ourselves. *I don't look like that when I wake up in my messy house with my ungrateful family who make it impossible for me to focus on my difficult job.*

For this reason, why not view social media with the same skeptical eye you view "reality" TV? We all know those shows are at least partly scripted, highly manipulated, expertly lit, directed for drama, and craftily edited to create a piece of entertainment.

Social media too is people presenting a part of themselves in a light that makes them feel good. Scripted, directed, edited.

Don't compare your real and raw life to that.

3. Comparing yourself to anyone else, ever

So ... don't compare your best to someone else's worst. You may have caught them at a bad moment.

And don't compare your worst to their best. Almost certainly it's a curated piece of self-presentation.

In fact, aim to stop comparing yourself to anyone else, ever.

One of the best things you can do to find happiness and self-respect is to *embrace your personal weirdness*. Sure, try to improve yourself in ways that matter to you, work toward your goals, cultivate your values. But meanwhile, *like* yourself.

Being an introvert, you have to spend an awful lot of time with you, in that head of yours. Comparing yourself with others — for better or worse — makes it harder to enjoy your own company and nurture your self-acceptance.

Thoughts of comparison are natural, and there's no point trying to pretend they won't pop into your head — they will. Don't resist. Don't engage. Just let them pop, then let them float away.

We all have days when we're kinda awesome and days when we suck like a turbo Dyson. Accept yourself for where you are, for the richness of your life and the complicated angels and demons of your personality. Accept others for where they are too. As much as possible, don't compare. You'll be a much happier introvert.

How To Recognize The 5 Stages Of Canceling Plans

Why do people make plans or accept invitations, only to cancel them at the last minute? It's so annoying! The question has vexed me for years, largely because I'm one of those annoying plan cancellers.

I've bought expensive tickets for events I was hugely excited to attend, RSVP'd yes to parties where I'd get to see beloved friends, even been the organizer for get-togethers of favorite people. But as the date approached I'd get sick, or somehow bring about some other emergency, or give away my ticket, or, if no one else was affected, simply not turn up.

Only recently have I worked out what's going on, and identified the stages I go through as I make and eventually break plans. So I thought I'd share my little insights in the hope that they save you some personal drama.

The Introvert's 5 Stages of Canceling Plans

Stage 1: Commitment

Recently a friend invited me to his birthday dinner.

Let me know where and I'll be there I texted back, upbeat and confident that I'd follow through on this simple and apparently pleasant thing.

But it was the start of a cycle I'd experienced many times before. A more observant person would have recognized the warm-up to this familiar dance. Not I. I would be quickstepping mindlessly for ages before recognizing the moves.

The problem, as I've now come to realize, is that Future Me is an extrovert. Future Me accepts invitations with gay abandon. Future Me suggests get-togethers when flush with affection for her friends. Future Me is genuinely excited by the prospect of these outings — she cannot imagine any change of mind, her desire to go is unequivocal. The further in the future, the more delightful the picture she plays in her mind. Heads thrown back in laughter, backs slapped. Happiness.

Of course Future Me never consults with Present Me, the one who must actually turn up. And Present Me is an extreme introvert.

As time passes and Present Me starts to emerge, things take a turn.

Stage 2: Seeking reassurance about the event

Once Present Me rears her head, there is often an attempt to gather more information. Questions about the guest list and location are asked, in an effort to lock down the style of the event and begin mental preparation.

Where will it take place? Who will be there? How many people? How many strangers? How crowded, how noisy, how likely the need for small talk? It's important to rule out some of the more alarming possibilities. Phrases that instantly raise the introvert's blood pressure include "communal restaurant tables" and "organized group activities".

If the guest list is small and the venue conducive to genuine and stimulating conversation, then the introvert is reassured. At this stage they may exit the Cancel cycle and proceed to actually attend the event. But if the venue is large, or conversation with over-friendly strangers likely, or if noise will limit conversation to small talk, then the introvert will become skittish.

At this point they may start to entertain fantasies of requiring surgery or being conscripted to top secret government work in order to have to stay home.

There is now a gradual coming to grips with the reality of the event, and a transition to the next stage.

Stage 3: Mild panic

As the introvert enters this stage they will seek evidence that the event may not proceed.

Often they'll use overcompensating joviality or an excess of punctuation and/or emoji in an attempt to hide the subterfuge. They might text:

Hey are you excited about your party?!? ?

In fact this is a veiled attempt to find out if there's any chance the event will be canceled. They're hoping to trigger a response along the lines of:

Actually I've had to cancel because (some benign reason).

The now slightly desperate introvert may even hope their message will subliminally manipulate the organizer to cancel the event:

Now that I think of it, it's probably a dumb idea to have a dinner for my birthday and invite all my friends. Your jovial enquiry has made me see the light. I shall cancel at once.

If notifications of cancellation are not forthcoming, then the introvert will shift into the next phase.

This transition is often swift and violent.

Stage 4: Blind terror and frantic attempts at escape

At this point the introvert will resemble a deer caught in headlights: immobilized, terrified, having no idea where to run.

They will see their situation clearly for the first time. The reality will dawn that they are well and truly cornered. Not only did they commit whole-heartedly to the occasion at the start, but they've now further trapped themselves by showing great anticipation.

Two possibilities will present themselves to the introvert:

1. Get sick

No, I don't mean say you're sick, I mean actually get sick.

This was my default strategy for many years before I understood that Future Me is an extrovert and will happily fill my diary with commitments I simply do not have the psychological resources to see through. Once in Stage 4, I'd wake up with a sore throat and fever. I'd go through boxes of aloe vera tissues, miss days of the gym and work. Quite often I would have the flu for two weeks.

When my near-delirium meant I had to cancel, my relief would be palpable. But I still didn't, in those days, connect the only-before-social-events illness with avoidance. Finally the pattern become so ridiculously obvious that Craig commented on it, and left me mentally racing back through years of social engagements thinking, *huh*.

As often happens when a psychological pattern switches from unconscious to conscious, things shifted, and I'm happy to say I no longer use this strategy.

2. 'Fess up

Instead, over time I've developed the willingness to explain that I'm hopeless at parties or big gatherings or whatever, and ask to be excused.

This has taken a lot of personal growth, as I haven't always had the clarity to understand what was going on for me, or the courage to be honest about it.

But I have very cool friends. Invariably, once I've plucked up my courage, crafted my explanation, parsed my explanatory text through a couple of beta readers, and sent my message, the response is warm and understanding.

Stage 5: Cancellation and relief

The final stage of canceling plans for the introvert is sheer, beautiful relief. Usually celebrated with the psychological equivalent of a magnum of champagne: an evening of carefully curated Netflix viewing. Possibly while drinking an actual magnum of champagne.

Recognizing the cycle of making plans, panicking, apologizing, and canceling plans has been life-changing for me. A major turning point was a Christmas event I went to a few years ago. A number of my friends were going to be there, so I RSVP'd "Yes!" and bought a fab dress and purchased my ticket. The closer it got, the more dread I felt, but I focused on the fact that I'd see my lovely friends.

Once I got there though, I found a loud, crowded venue. It was impossible to have a conversation — at least for me. I had to yell, which I hate, and I said "pardon" so many times that eventually I just gave up and started nodding periodically, having no idea what I was agreeing with.

After about twenty minutes I couldn't take it anymore. I snuck out, found a taxi, got the driver to stop at KFC, messaged Craig to say I was miserable and coming home with a bucket of chicken. As I cradled my bucket and inhaled the secret herbs and spices in the taxi, I realized, *This is who I am*. I don't like disappointing people but I just can't be different and it's so exhausting to try.

I still occasionally fall into to the trap of letting that socially promiscuous trollop Future Me commit me to too many or too large engagements, or too many of them too close together. As I did recently with my friend's birthday dinner.

But my friends are pretty cool, and it's usually no surprise to them when I pull out. And then we make a smaller, more intimate date.

And those I always keep.

How To Deal With Intrusive People

At a recent hairdresser appointment I had a classic introvert experience.

A sweet shampoo girl offered me "a relaxing hand massage" while my conditioning treatment worked its magic. How perfect, I thought, conjuring visions of a lovely massage, aromatic scents wafting about me, as I blissed out into a peaceful coma. "Relaxing" was built right into the description — what could go wrong?

So I accepted gratefully, extended my hand, closed my eyes, lay back in the chair, and prepared to enjoy this little oasis of serenity.

But just as my mind began to swirl with the pleasure of the scented cream and a smile started to spread across my face, I was jolted from my reverie.

"So do you have children?"

I opened my eyes to find the girl seated very close beside me, staring intently at me, leaning forward eagerly as she massaged. And by "massaged" I mean held my hand and periodically squeezed.

"Um, no," I said simply. I thought if I gave a minimal response and closed my eyes again, she would get the hint. I leaned back into the reclined chair.

"Oh really. Why's that? Are you planning to?"

"Um, not sure," I murmured. Which technically isn't a lie.

"Do you have brothers and sisters?"

I started to perspire. This was not going well. I now realized "relaxing hand massage" was a cruelly misleading advertisement for this ordeal. In fact "relaxing hand massage" meant this girl would sit beside me, bore into my soul with her eyes, and gulf-stream a barrage of questions at me. While intermittently caressing my hand.

Like many introverts, I loathe small talk. I don't mind talking to a stranger if there's a natural connection, an unforced point of mutual interest that happens spontaneously, organically. In fact, friends have accused me of being flirtatious because I'll happily and sometimes deeply engage with service staff when shopping, or with wait staff at a restaurant, because we've made a genuine connection over something. Shoes or handbags or wine, usually.

But if I am required to chit-chat, and especially if I have to answer personal questions from someone I don't already know and like, it's a form of torture, second only to ice-breaker activities at a team-building weekend away. And doubly awful because there's not the promise of imminent cocktails to ease the pain.

Another time I recently felt this same sense of being trapped and psychologically invaded was at the gym. A fellow class participant who I don't personally know approached me after class and fired a series of questions at me.

What classes do you do?
Why do you do those?
Why do you do that stretch?
How long have you been coming here?
What is your diet?

None of these are questions I mind answering. But I feel decidedly antagonistic toward a stranger who asks me questions in this intrusive way. I answered, but I felt cranky for some days after this exchange.

I realized later that the reason I felt put out was largely my own fault.

You see, I had answered about myself, explaining why I do things the way I do, and sharing my personal approach. I barely knew the woman — of course it felt intrusive and unpleasant.

Instead, I should have turned the questions around. I should have asked what her goals were and suggested classes that would help her achieve those. I should have said I do the classes and stretches that feel right for me, and that she should do what feels right for her.

I should have focused on answering what she needed to know for her, not on giving up excessive information about me.

It's that laser focus on us that can be so unpleasant for introverts.

Thankfully, I handled things slightly better at the hairdresser. Realizing there would be no end to the questioning onslaught, I sadly surrendered my relaxing-hand-massage fantasy and salvaged what I could of my inner peace. Which meant not passively letting the questions assail me. Which meant taking charge and turning the questioning tables.

"Do you have brothers and sisters?" I asked.

Each answer opened the door to another question I could ask.

How old are they?

Do you all live at home?

Who does the cooking?

She answered chattily and happily. Smiling and laughing as she shared little stories about her family.

Did I feel like a phony asking questions I had zero interest in? You betcha.

But it was better than facing the question fusillade and reaching emotional boiling point, and eventually either snapping at her or holding it in and later snapping at someone whose only fault was to ask if I knew where Pottery Barn was.

I'm grateful for both these experiences, though, as they've helped me develop a strategy for dealing with strangers who question you intrusively. Or in a way that feels intrusive to introverts.

First, work out what the other person is looking for — information to help their own goals, social interaction, whatever — and try to provide it in a way that doesn't make your introverted self feel psychologically violated.

Second, keep the focus on the other person by asking them questions.

Third and most importantly, never be drawn in by the offer of a "relaxing hand massage". You will regret it.

How To Cultivate Stay-At-Home Style

If you're an introvert then you probably spend a fair amount of time at home. Reading. Watching your favorite shows. Writing or being artistic. Thinking. Learning. Pottering around. Decompressing. Pretending not to be home if (*what horror is this!?*) someone unexpectedly knocks. Generally hanging with, you know, yourself.

But just because you're *at* home doesn't mean you have to *look* homely.

Be a Homebody, not a Homely Body

Over the years I've found what I wear at home has a surprising effect on what I do and how I feel. It can dramatically shift my mood and motivation. For instance:

- If my clothes are baggy I tend to snack waaaaay more.

- If I wouldn't wear it in public I feel kinda yucky wearing it in private.
- If my clothes are shapeless my posture is sloppier.
- If there's no style to my outfit I find it harder to get motivated to work.
- If I'm well-groomed and well-dressed — even in a simple, at-home way — it brightens my mood and makes me feel happier.

You may relate to some of my observations. Or maybe you don't, but you've noticed your own correlations between what you wear and how you feel.

But!

While it might boost your mood and motivation to kick your at-home style up a notch, you don't want to complicate your morning routine. We introverts do enough overthinking as it is!

So what's the solution? How do you balance comfort and cuteness? How do you add a little style without giving yourself something *more* to overanalyze?

My Sofa-Chic "Uniform"

Well, here's my approach:

1. I've gotten rid of every item of clothing from my closet that is tatty, ill-fitting, uncomfortable, or in a color, shape, or style that doesn't suit me.

Just let them go. Even if never worn. Even if expensive. Gone. That has simplified my daily choices.

2. I've made it a habit to wash my face, brush my teeth, tidy my hair, dress neatly, put on lip balm, and make the bed before I face the day. Even if the day involves seeing no one but *moi*.

3. I've developed a routine of shifting going-out clothes into staying-home rotation once I've worn them what feels like "enough" times.

4. I've developed a kind of at-home uniform of black yoga or gym pants and black fitted tank tops. I have several of each that all mix and match. If it's cold I add Ugg boots*, which I update about every two years so they stay snug and neat. I really feel the cold so I have sweaters and hoodies in ascending levels of warmth that I progress through as the seasons cool. (*Never worn outside my apartment. Not-at-home style matters too! Even to introverts.)

This makes dressing every morning a breeze, as everything is comfortable, everything matches, and everything has some structure so I feel "dressed".

It's relaxed enough for quality *sofa* time, yet *chic* enough for me to feel alert and motivated. Hence my name for this at-home dress style: *sofa chic*.

Dressing this way allows me to tap-tap-tap at my desk, sit cross-legged in my armchair for reading or research, potter around my apartment, curl up on the sofa to watch my stories, or answer the door when the pizza dude arrives — all while feeling comfortable and presentable.

Creating your own Sofa-Chic Style

So how do you create your own version of sofa chic? Here are some suggestions:

1. Consider what you do when you're at home

If you need to feel motivated to work, then choose something with a little structure. If you like to cross your legs to read or write or to curl up on the sofa, then choose something with some give. If you feel the cold, then choose something snug and cozy.

2. Pick clothes that mix and match so you don't have to overthink your choices

It's easy to feel overwhelmed as an introvert, so consider whether a few key neutral colors can form the basis of your wardrobe — perhaps black, white, and navy; or cream, camel, and chocolate. This simplifies life and also looks great in your closet too.

3. Dress for you

The idea is to feel happy and presentable, to avoid feeling slobby or sloppy, which can undermine your self-esteem. Maybe it's jeans and T-shirts. Maybe it's cute dresses and cardigans. Maybe it's pants and button-down shirts. Decide what *you* like to wear. This is for you, not for anyone else.

4. Don't tell yourself it's fine to wear something tatty or ill-fitting just because you're at home

For introverts, home is one of the best places to be! So decide to donate or toss anything that doesn't look and feel good. Have only quality stuff to choose from for your at-home wardrobe.

5. Realize it's not a waste to look nice, even when no one else is there to see it

You know how you feel. *You* see yourself in the mirror. So of course it's worth wearing something nice and taking care with your appearance. You spend a lot of time with you — show yourself some respect!

As introverts we cherish quality time at home. It's not simply time *between* things we want to do. It's *pleasurable* time, when we enjoy our own company and engage in our interests and artistic pursuits and nerd pastimes.

Taking care of yourself and feeling happy is good for your heart and mind — not to mention good for all your relationships. So wear what looks and feels comfortable and presentable to you. And feel great about having an attractive at-home style.

How To Leave A Party Early

Many introverts don't enjoy parties. *Because they're parties.* But what if attending a party is really important to someone you care about, and it's worth mustering the psychological resources to get yourself there? Do you have to stay until the last person leaves?

Well, guess what? No!

So then how do you extricate yourself? Here's how to do it with grace.

How to Leave a Party Early with Grace

1. Don't lie

One option is to make up an excuse.
I have an early meeting tomorrow.
The dog needs to be walked.
The CIA is waiting at my house.
But that's no way to live, telling lies to avoid being who you are. Over time it will erode your self-esteem and your relationships.

2. Don't whine

Another option is to plaintively over-explain. To launch into a longwinded account of how you're really uncomfortable at parties and you get super anxious and it all began when you were a child …

But that isn't going to leave you feeling good either, especially if the host wisely starts to nod off in the middle of your saga.

3: Do be honest and keep it simple

Yep, the best way to handle parties is to be honest and to keep it simple. It's fine to be self-deprecating, but don't insult or disrespect yourself.

Here's my 3-step formula:

3 Steps to Leaving a Party Early

Step 1: When you RSVP, say upfront that you'll be leaving early

If possible, RSVP by text or email so you can finesse your wording.

Try something like:

I'm not a party person so will head off around 9 pm. But I'm looking forward to celebrating with you!

I'd love to see you and drop by with your gift. I'll just stay an hour.

Now you've set expectations about how long you'll stay, making step 2 much easier.

Step 2A: If appropriate, simply slip away

If it's a large party and the host is busy, just slip out. The host has enough going on. Your saying goodbye might make them feel like they should encourage you to stay. Plus, you've already explained that you'll leave early so there's no need to make a big deal.

If you get stopped by another guest and asked why you're leaving early, just deflect the focus:

Wasn't it a beautiful ceremony?

Didn't George look great in his purple velour suit?

How about that paleo cake!

Then give them a smile and be on your way to that pleasure dome known as home.

Step 2B: If it's a small affair or dinner party and you can't slip away, use my patented Restroom Segue

Excuse yourself to go to the restroom. That will give you a moment to collect yourself and already be on your feet, plus it lets the evening start to move on without you. Honestly, it's genius.

When you return, gather up your coat and purse or whatever on the way back to the host.

Then you can simply appear, coat in hand, and say something like:

Well, George and Martha, thank you for a lovely evening.

If you're entreated to stay, say thank you and immediately deflect the focus off yourself with something positive but true about the food, company, venue, decor, wine, whatever. A genuine compliment is a lovely way to mark your exit.

Oh you're very kind. Those cocktails were amazing! Goodnight, everyone.

Thank you so much. Oh and I love the table settings — so elegant. Goodnight.

Step 3: Accept that some people might not like it

With some people it won't matter what you say, they'll be offended. Possibly the host, possibly a guest, possibly the caterer who saw you secrete that canapé into the hibiscus syriacus foliage.

You can't please everyone and also be whole and true to yourself. People are too different and have their own stuff going on and don't always understand. All you can do is be kind and respectful to yourself and gracious to your host and fellow guests, and let the chips fall where they may.

And if someone gets cross and hurls a bowl of

snacks at you, then also let those chips fall where they may. There'll be a lot of cleaning up to do tomorrow anyway.

How To Avoid Phone Calls

Remember the 2002 horror flick *The Ring*? How the *brring-brring* of the telephone preempts a supernatural abomination? How a phone call is a source of unutterable terror, a portent of evil, an instrument of doom?

This is totally what it's like for introverts.

Introverts and Phone-Hate

Why do introverts hate talking on the phone?

These days it's common to avoid the phone and even voicemail, with many people preferring the convenience and time-shifting of text and apps. For introverts though, phone calls can hold an added dread.

Partly, I think, it's the noise, the piercing of a peaceful quiet. Evidence shows introverts are more sensitive to sounds.

Partly it's the intensity. There's no escape — you're just kind of stuck until the call ends. This is the worst part for me. I don't like feeling I can't get away.

Partly it's the absence of visual cues. I feel much more comfortable when I can see a person's face, and especially their eyes, as I talk to them.

Then there's the horror of the voicemail asking you to return a call. It's bad enough if someone explains why they're calling. But what about people who say, *Hey it's me — can you give me a call?* That's the worst, because you don't know whether they're bored and simply want to chat or something awful has happened and they need you. So frustrating!

I've never enjoyed chatting on the phone and this has sometimes been an issue in my relationships. Just as I hate the phone, others love it.

As I've gotten older though, I've found I can only really sustain relationships with people I see in person and/or can connect with online or via text or email. Life is short. Too often phone calls aren't.

How to De-Phone-Call your personal life

If you'd like to protect yourself from phone-talk fatigue as well as weird Japanese necromancy a la *The Ring* and even neatly-plotted attempted homicide as in *Dial M for Murder*, the following tips might help.

These are some of the ways I've de-phone-called my personal life:

- When filling out contact details I give my email address rather than phone number whenever possible.

- When sharing phone numbers with a new friend I say upfront that I don't answer my phone and prefer to text.
- I keep my ringer turned off. I write for a living and hate losing focus to a ringing telephone.
- I have "Just Can't Get Enough" as a ringtone. That way if the phone does ring, I can simply forget that it's a call and dance until the music stops.
- I keep the phone app hidden on about page 4 and off my home screen.
- If I see a missed call from a friend I text them and ask what's up. I'm always friendly but I don't over-explain the phone-avoidance thing.
- In general I promptly return my friends' emails and texts. That way, they know they can reach me quickly via these options.

And best of all? My entire voicemail message consists of three words: *Please text me*.

How To Design Your Ideal Morning Routine (Even If You're Not A Morning Person)

If you're a ~~space alien~~ morning person then you can save yourself some time and stop reading now. There's nothing here for you, with your bouncing out of bed and your chirpy *Good morning!* and your ability to navigate the world wholly uncaffeinated.

But if you're like me, an easily overstimulated introvert who is often all peopled out; if every morning is like a difficult birth, a cruel expulsion from the warm womb of your bed into a harsh, rambunctious, over-lit reality that expects you to function as an adult and operate the coffee machine and be civil *before midday*; then read on.

For there is a secret to making your transition from dreamy to dexterous a calmer one, involving fewer expletives, hardly any tantrums, and considerably less broken crockery. The secret is to have a morning routine.

Why have a Morning Routine?

The morning routine works for three main reasons.

First, it is a routine, a set order of steps, a series of actions that occur on autopilot. This removes the great enemy of the newly awake brain: *decision-making*. The decisions have been pre-made — the scrambled mind need only follow the routine. Very little thinking is required. Which is perfect, because at that point very little thinking is pretty much all we're capable of.

Second, it protects you in your fragile state from known irritants in the outside world — from annoying people who expect you to speak in coherent sentences through to information that requires active brain cells for processing. A morning routine lets you slowly build up your stamina before you have to cope with such grueling demands.

Third, it sets you up well for the day. You check in with yourself. You're more conscious. You clarify what matters, what you want from yourself.

Sounds good, right? So what are the elements of the ideal morning routine?

What is the Perfect Morning Routine?

Here's my 7-step prescription for a great morning routine.

1. Stretch, rise, throw back the covers

While still in bed, take a moment to gloriously extend your limbs, neck, ankles, wrists, hips, torso. I find it helps to moan and carry on a bit, really drawing out the pleasure of streeeeeetching your body. It feels nice — enjoy it!

Next, get out of bed and throw back those covers. This step lets your bed breathe for a while and signals that you have left the womb. Ta da! We are bleary eyed and vague, but we have emerged. It is the cutting of the cord. But less ew.

2. Defer devices

I can see the terror in your eyes as you read this but trust me, avoiding the internet is key. In your delicate condition, difficult news or a troubling email or an ambiguous comment on social media can instantly wreck your mood or cause you to completely overreact (this has *never* happened to me) and set you up for a cranky day.

I know you'll be tempted — we all are. Although I've been using this morning ritual for many months now, I still fight the urge to grab my phone and sneak a somnambulant check-in. But unless you're right on the verge of curing cancer or ending poverty and every update matters, resist. Just try it for a few days and see how you feel.

3. Make yourself a delicious breakfast

For me breakfast is piping hot, grainy toast with melty butter and a strong flat white. I've been having the same breakfast for years and I just love it. I've worked out the timing so the coffee and toast get ready at the same time, like an operatic crescendo of rising harmonies. (It's possible I *may* be overly dramatic about my breakfast.)

As a Sunday ritual Craig and I treat ourselves to large, oven-warmed croissants with butter and raspberry confiture, and of course coffee.

This is not the time to force-feed yourself kale smoothies (unless they make you feel good). This is the time to enjoy something nourishing and delicious. Something good for your body *and* mind.

4. Do something enjoyable while you have breakfast

What would make breakfast time more pleasant for you?

I complete the *Sydney Morning Herald* quick crossword on my iPad (the crossword is on a timer, which keeps me disciplined about staying off email and social media). It's fun, and as a writer I like having a daily vocabulary challenge.

I know people who love to sit on their balconies and watch the world wake up, or who feel stimulated by reading a motivational book, or some who even talk to family members, which seems awfully brave and foolhardy to me, but to each their own.

Don't use this time to stress yourself out over email or yell at people on Facebook or howl at the state of the world. You can do all that later.

Note: If you have family or housemates who expect to engage with you at this time, consider resetting expectations. No need to make a big thing of it, simply say something like:

I've noticed I'm crabby in the morning so I want to try a new morning ritual and see how that works. I'm going to sit in the spare room by myself and have my cereal and read a novel for fifteen minutes every morning.

If you have little ones and a partner, you could each take turns to get your fifteen minutes.

If you have little ones and no partner, you may have to *DUN DUN DUN!* leave the ~~womb~~ bed earlier. I'm no fan of rising any earlier than strictly necessary but I think this may just be worth it.

5. Have an inspiring morning activity

Next, spend some time — five, ten, twenty minutes, whatever you can manage — doing something that motivates or inspires you, or clarifies what's important to you right now. Something that sets a good direction for your day, for what you want to achieve and how you'd like to comport yourself.

For me, this is my version of Julia Cameron's morning pages. (In the wonderful book *The Artist's Way*, Cameron prescribes a creative practice of three handwritten, stream-of-consciousness pages, to be done first thing each morning.) It's a kind of self-therapy where I write with abandon about whatever — it could be downloading something swirling around in my brain, troubleshooting a personal or professional problem, giving myself a pep talk, ~~horrendously overanalyzing something trivial,~~ exploring an idea — anything at all. I never censor myself and I never re-read (I couldn't if I wanted to, as my scrawl is indecipherable, composed entirely of such brilliant nuggets as "harden of antelope Toblerone"). Regardless, I use a beautiful Lamy pen and Moleskine journal, so the process is rather lovely.

Many people like to do a meditation practice, which is a fine idea. Sadly my attempts at meditation have not been successful and have usually involved my screaming at various people and inanimate objects to be quiet so I could be serene in peace.

6. Make the bed

Making your bed is one of those tiny, undervalued tasks that more than returns the time and effort it takes, giving you a precious feeling of peace and order. It makes going to bed that night a much nicer experience too.

After a couple of weeks of bed-making you'll be able to whip through it in about three minutes. It looks good, it feels good.

Make the bed even if you live alone. Even if no one else in your home appreciates it (they probably won't). Even if you think it's a waste of time because you'll only mess it up again tonight. *Even still.*

If you aren't a regular bed-maker then it may feel like unnecessary work for a couple of weeks. Persevere. If you're not convinced by the end of that time, set yourself free from this step.

7. Dress your best

Whether you spend your days walking the catwalk or cleaning the kitty litter, take care in your self-presentation. Wear flattering clothes, do something you like with your hair, cultivate a good posture. Carry an attractive handbag or satchel. Have a little style.

Why? Because you'll feel ready for the day, you'll feel *bien dans sa peau* — a lovely French expression that means "feeling good in your skin". Wouldn't you like to go about your day feeling good in your skin?

Bien sûr, you whisper breathlessly, all Jane Birkin, as you start thinking about your own morning routine. Why, you little minx, you!

How To Avoid The Introvert Versus Extrovert Trap

People like Susan Cain have done a lot to make "introvert" and "extrovert" mainstream concepts. This is great — it means more self-awareness, self-acceptance, and happiness for everyone. Or so you'd think.

But I've noticed negative backlash — people feeling superior for being one or the other, or putting others down.

This is a common trap when you identify with a group — whether a sports team, profession, gender, phone brand, or anything that lets your brain say *us* versus *them*. It's all too easy to feel competitive or threatened or intolerant. The same efficient brain processes that help us simplify a complex world can also make us vulnerable to unhelpful us-versus-them thinking.

Here are good reasons to avoid getting caught in the extrovert-versus-introvert trap.

4 Reasons to Avoid the Introvert versus Extrovert Trap

1. There's no pure introvert or extrovert

Extroversion and introversion are not binary, mutually exclusive concepts like black and white. Rather, they are extremes of a single continuum.

Everybody, and I mean everybody, is a shade of gray.

You and I both fall somewhere along this introversion-extroversion spectrum, closer to one end or the other, or somewhere in the middle (an ambivert). No one is pure extrovert or introvert.

And there's more. Not only are these concepts ends of a single notion, but they are also themselves multifaceted.

Introversion, as psychologists use the term today, is not a single unified trait, but a statistically identified collection of narrower sub-traits that include level of sociability, energy, activity, sensation-seeking, interpersonal dominance, and tendency to experience positive emotional states. Two people could fall at the same level of introversion based on a personality test, but they could be completely different on each of these underlying sub-traits.

So introversion and extroversion are relative tendencies rather than absolutes. And they are broad concepts that contain narrow traits. Therefore it makes little sense to see the world in us-and-them, introvert-versus-extrovert distinctions. It's just not that simple.

2. Personality is greater than extroversion and introversion

Another important reason to avoid the introvert versus extrovert trap is that there's more to the way psychologists view personality.

The introversion-extroversion scale can be described in general terms as a biologically based preference for more or less stimulation — which could be light or noise or socializing. Introverts like less stimulation to feel comfortable and extroverts like more stimulation to feel comfortable.

But this is only one of the "Big Five" statistically identified components of personality, as we discussed in *How To Understand The Psychology Of Introverts*.

Seeing people simplistically as introverts or extroverts, as though that sums them up, omits other important aspects of who we are.

3. Understanding extroversion and introversion helps you accept yourself

So if the concept of introvert-extrovert is so relative and broad, and only part of the personality picture, then what makes it important?

That's a good question. Especially as this entire book is about introverts! Here's why it matters.

Of the "Big Five" personality components, introversion-extroversion is the one with the most potential to affect your self-acceptance and happiness. Why?

Because being an introvert *and not knowing you're an introvert* can leave you feeling like there's something very wrong with you.

It can make you feel like a failure at work if you can't concentrate in an open-plan office. It can make you feel like a misanthrope if you love your friends but need a lot of time to yourself. It can make you wonder what your problem is that you're sensitive to noise and light — and, well, many things.

Extroverts by their nature are more visible, more *out there* than introverts. Extroverts are who we hear in meetings and see in movies and observe in the media. They become our idea of the norm. This means people who are introverted can feel like misfits. They can spend their lives trying to fit in and become something they're not.

None of the other "Big Five" personality components have so much potential to change how you see yourself, to affect the decisions you make in your life, and to make you happier.

Discovering I'm an at the extreme end of introversion and changing my life to accommodate this reality has been the single greatest adjustment of my adult life. It has liberated my work, improved my relationships, and turned self-doubt into self-acceptance. It has brought me joy.

And that's why I wrote this book — the hope that others would enjoy more happiness too.

4. Understanding introversion and extroversion helps you accept others

The consequence of understanding yourself better and cutting yourself some personality slack is that you also do this for others.

This is the price of self-knowledge: you must also understand others better, too.

Since finding out I'm an introvert and, over time, coming to accept and now love this part of myself, I've become much more tolerant of other people as well.

Accepting my love of staying in has given me so much more understanding of friends who love to party. Cultivating my passion for nerdy pastimes and hobbies has stopped me feeling disconnected from people who love sports or adventure activities. Yes, even campers. Indulging my preference for low-noise and low-light environments has made me more respectful of others' preference for brightness and volume.

Accepting myself has opened me up to accept others.

More Acceptance and Happiness for Everybody

In short, the single, broad, and very *gray* continuum of introversion-extroversion is nothing more than *information*.

It's counterproductive to use this information to judge others or as an excuse to feel superior. As we've seen, introverts and extroverts are not on separate teams or in discrete silos — we're all just swimming in different depths of the same gray.

But if recognizing our relative differences helps us accept ourselves more, then let's embrace those differences. Let's cultivate our strengths and indulge our preferences and enjoy our pleasures.

And let's consciously nurture the other side of this too — a greater acceptance of other people's strengths and preferences and pleasures.

Let's use what we learn about extroversion and introversion to enjoy less "them versus us" and more "different kinds of us".

Part 3: The Delightful Hilarity of Being an Introvert

We're all a little weird. And life is a little weird. And when we find someone whose weirdness is compatible with ours, we join up with them and fall into mutually satisfying weirdness—and call it love—true love.

—*Robert Fulghum, True Love*

The Adventures Of Kurt The Introverted Donkey: Kurt And The Donkey Shell

There once was an introverted little donkey named Kurt.

When Kurt was a young, up-and-coming corporate donkey he used to try to fit in with his donkey colleagues.

He attended donkey shindigs and chatted lots of donkey talk. If he wanted to leave a party early and the other donkeys stopped him, he agreed to stay. He always tried to be nice and go along with what the other donkeys encouraged him to do.

But poor Kurt felt exhausted and miserable. He did not enjoy himself. He tried not to let it show, but inside he wanted to bray and bray and bray.

After a while Kurt couldn't keep it in any longer and he became a very cranky little donkey. The other donkeys did not like this.

Why so crotchety Kurt? they asked. *What's with the resting jennet face? Why are you always in a mood?*

What was Kurt to do? He wanted to get along with his colleagues so he decided to take a little time out and calm himself down.

He spent time alone. He said no to donkey parties and avoided donkey chit-chat.

Instead, he read donkey books (Donkey Juan) and watched donkey shows (Game of Mules) and ate donkey snacks (his favorite tortilla chips, Burro-itos). He even tried his hoof at some very fine donkey calligraphy.

He still spent time with his closest donkey pals, Herb and Lamont. And he texted with a cute girl-donkey he liked, Clarissa. No donkey pics though, for Kurt was a gentle donkey.

Soon he felt better and happier. He was much less cranky. His resting jennet face was gone.

However, some of the other donkeys were not pleased. They thought he should not spend so much time at home.

What's wrong Kurt? they asked. *You should come out of your donkey shell. You need to get out more.*

Little Kurt pondered this dilemma.

If he didn't get enough time to himself he felt unhappy.

If he did get enough time to himself the other donkeys were not happy.

Kurt realized he couldn't be happy and also make all the other donkeys happy — he had to choose.

So he chose what made him happy.

He chose to listen to his own little donkey heart and spend time alone, time with his pals, and only a little time going to donkey shindigs.

He chose to leave the parties he did attend early by slipping out quietly, which is not easy to do when you're a donkey and your tail tends to wipe out entire trays of canapés and also smash delicate light fittings.

After a while the donkeys reacted to this new Kurt.

Some of the donkeys judged Kurt and claimed he must hate donkeys. They brayed behind his back and didn't invite him to things out of spite. They didn't get the irony.

Some of the donkeys understood Kurt and were happy to enjoy his company when he was around. They realized that just as they liked noise and people and socializing, he liked quiet and solitude and close friends.

Some of the donkeys felt emboldened by Kurt, and decided to be more true to themselves as well. Mavis adjusted her tool belt and declared: *I like jennets!* (The other donkeys tried to look surprised.) Steve left the company to pursue his true passion, studying pharmacology. (He'd always wanted to be a drug mule.)

The moral of this story is that no matter what you do, someone will think you're an ass.

But you may as well be a happy ass.

Which means you need to find your own balance and respect your inner donkey self. And that can be done very well from inside your donkey shell.

Advice Column: Ask The Introvert Sage

Pity Party

Dear Introvert Sage,

Sometimes my colleagues ask if I have plans for the weekend, and when I say I plan to stay in and watch Netflix and practice my cursive writing, they make sad faces and invite me out with them. I'm confused. Are they jealous? What is happening?

Netflix & Quill

Dear Netflix & Quill,

Given the near-indecipherability of the penmanship in your letter I commend your well-chosen weekend agenda. As for your confusion, what is happening is that your colleagues believe your delightful plans to be tragic non-plans. What is happening is *pity*.

The solution is to tell them of your plans but translate

it into their language. A fair rendering might be:

> I shall participate in a boisterous group sport and later attend a raucous party precluding meaningful conversation. The following day I shall join a large assortment of gentlefolk as they assemble for a poorly organized picnic in an overcrowded area and partake of a great surfeit of potato salad.

(I believe I have the lingo down but you may care to make your own edits.)

They will understand this to mean you have plans and will not feel compelled to include you in theirs. Do write again once you have the ink spills and smudges under control.

Being Shellfish

> Dear Introvert Sage
>
> People keep telling me to come out of my shell. It's very annoying, because I feel they just want me to be conventionally social so they feel more comfortable. How do I get them to back off?
>
> Shelly

Dear Shelly,

Is that your real name? Because I make the jokes here, just so you know.

Your solution is simple. Instead of getting *them* to back off, take your *own* back off.

Invest in a Teenage Mutant Ninja Turtle costume and wear it *everywhere*. Work, shopping, society weddings. When people tell you to come out of your shell, simply remove the costume. *Voilà!*

PRO TIP: Remember to wear underwear.

Sigh High Club

Dear Introvert Sage,

I travel for work and always have earbuds, iPad, books and magazines to entertain myself on flights. Yet the person next to me invariably ignores my multiple "please don't talk to me" signals and pesters me with small talk throughout the flight. It makes me want to slam my tray table into the upright position. Am I responsible for entertaining them?

Sigh High Club Member

Dear Sigh High Club Member,

Ah yes, the person who expects a seat-mate to provide their inflight entertainment ...

The solution is to have a selection of entertainments on your person that you can brandish as soon as an attempt is made to penetrate your cone of silence.

Great choices are *Where's Wally*, join-the-dots or coloring books (remember the crayons!), and Nietzsche's *Thus Spoke Zarathustra*. Simply place the selection on their tray table, wish them a good flight, and turn back to your own reading material.

If they persist in prattling at you, simply use two fingers of each hand to point helpfully at the materials as well as the exits.

Won't Take a Hint

Dear Introvert Sage,

A colleague at work keeps stopping by my desk and chattering nonstop. I try looking at my watch and yawning, but she just won't take hints. My jaw is starting to hurt. Help!

All Yawned Out

Dear All Yawned Out,

I had the exact same problem. My workmate would trap me at my desk and yabber tirelessly, apparently having mastered circular breathing, as there was never a pause where I could say I needed to get back to work. Like you, I tried the watch, the yawn, the glazed expression — but nothing got through.

Finally I happened upon a solution. I simply reached for my desk phone, started dialing a number (it was the local pizzeria) and put the call on speaker so the ringing phone could be heard. Of course I maintained eye contact with her as I did this — I didn't want to appear *rude*. She kept talking throughout. When my call was answered, I gently lifted the handset and turned away to start the call.

There was a lot of discussion about toppings and cheese options and potential stuffed crusts and eventually she left, otherwise I fear she would be standing at that desk and talking still.

PS: I did ask if she liked anchovies — I'm not an animal.

Canceled Plans

> Dear Introvert Sage,
>
> I get a real frisson of joy when plans get canceled. Is there something wrong with me?
>
> Daphlette

Dear Daphlette,

Your parents have made up a ridiculous name so yes, very likely there is something congenitally wrong with you. But that is beyond the purview of my column.

However I can help with the canceled plans. Find a coterie of like-minded introverts and form a "social club". Stop laughing, Daphlette — I didn't laugh at your name. Well, I did, but who's the sage here? ANYWAY form this social club and organize a series of events — parties, dinners, weekends away, abseiling classes.

Then, just as each event approaches, cancel it. Everyone will be thrilled and delighted and you, the architect of the constant frissons, will be considered a hero.

The Introvert's 9 Circles Of Hell

Ever wondered what hell would be like for introverts? I think it would be something like this ...

Abandon all hope, ye introverts who enter here ...

Dante, kind of

Circle 1: Networking

In this circle the introvert souls writhe and groan as they are forced to shake hands, drink coffee out of urns, and listen to people talk about being disruptors.

They howl in wretchedness and engage in small talk while dressed in smart casual attire.

Circle 2: Garrulous People

Here the introvert souls are trapped in an everlasting fire with a taxi driver, dentist, or massage therapist who talks nonstop.

Unable to escape the scorching verbal flames, the introvert souls are ceaselessly required to answer questions about where they live or what they do or what they think about random bland topics.

Circle 3: Organized Activities

Circle 3 is where the introvert souls are tortured in a seething underworld of group activities.

Their strength is pushed to the very limits of endurance as they engage en masse in games, ice-breakers, trust exercises, and other ordeals of group damnation.

Circle 4: Group Projects

Here the tormented introvert souls are condemned to complete tasks with other people, despite being willing to do all the work themselves in exchange for being allowed to work alone.

Fallen angels, heretics, and bossy loudmouths dominate every discussion while contributing no actual work. The sullen ones gurgle beneath the waters. And also contribute no actual work.

Circle 5: People Who Can't/Won't Read Cues

In this circle the introvert souls are trapped in a nightmare world where people refuse to acknowledge the universal signals of *Please leave me alone*.

These wicked torturers ignore obvious earbuds, open books, dark sunglasses, closed body language, and eye contact avoidance. Instead, they firmly tap shoulders, smile and wave jovially in faces, and obliviously talk and talk and talk at the squirming and twisting introvert souls. The introvert souls are hurled about in this violent storm with no hope of rest.

Circle 6: Crowded Shopping Centers

In this foul swamp introvert souls must wander from level to level of the abyss, jostled endlessly by people with no sense of personal space.

Here is found a bottomless pit of sales and seasonal clearances, where things lacking appeal at full price are hurled at the avaricious and the prodigal, who screech and grasp and surrender all dignity in exchange for discounted items they do not need and have no room for. Also called limbo.

Circle 7: Having to Answer the Phone

In this nether world the miserable introvert souls are encased in flaming tombs, also known as automatically answered telephone headsets.

Without hope of peace, the accursed introverts wander amid the thieves, liars, cheats, sorcerers, false prophets, and those who post too many selfies, forever blown about by vile winds and unavoidable telephone calls.

Circle 8: Unnecessary Space Invaders

The introvert souls in this circle are condemned for all eternity to be in uncrowded places yet have noisy, vexatious persons disregard the many available seats and sit very close by.

In this pit of perdition the noisy ones talk loudly, ignorantly, and incessantly. Their ignored children thrash about and scream in hellish agony, for absolutely no reason at all.

Circle 9: Satan's Personal Pad

Here is the lowest and most terrifying level, the grim depths of hell, dominated by the salivating, ever-devouring mouths of Satan.

Also known as Ikea.

Introvert Movie Database: If Famous Films Were About Introverts

The typical movie protagonist is totally out there — being adventurous, socializing with less-attractive, quip-making friends, probably not spending a lot of on-screen time reading books or doing puzzles.

But let me ask you this: Have you ever wondered how differently events would unfold if a movie protagonist were an introvert?

Me neither! At least until now. Here's how I think movies in the "Introvert Movie Database" might go …

Titanic

An introverted woman cannot think of anything worse than being trapped on a ship with thousands of strangers and forced into small talk. She decides instead to stay home and read, and meets a cute guy at the bookstore when they both reach for a hardcover on icebergs. They find true love and no one dies and no Celine Dion is played. The End.

Frozen

Introverted princess has cryokinetic powers. Parents confine her to her room until she can wield her ice magic with greater control. She enjoys the solitude and makes no effort to improve, happy to stay in her room with her laptop and icicle art. A typical introvert, she has a tendency to overthink things so sings "Let It Go" to herself. Otherwise she is content. The End.

Casablanca

An expatriate American has a busy nightclub in Casablanca. As an introvert he finds the club too noisy, crowded, and rambunctious. Consequently he hires a small office in a quiet part of town where he does accounts, weekly orders, and staff payroll. He never hears the words "letters of transit". He used to love a girl during the war but rarely thinks of her now. He develops a lovely bromance with a local police captain, another introvert whom he meets at a screening of *The Usual Suspects*. The End.

The Sixth Sense

Introverted kid sees dead people but won't speak to them because he doesn't like strangers. Especially dead ones. The kid has a sixth sense that the dead people will eventually give up on him. They do. The End.

Strangers On A Train

Two people, both with a motive to kill someone in their lives, take the same long train journey. As they are both introverts they have books, phones, iPads, and earbuds to help them avoid contact with strangers. They never speak, remaining forever strangers on a train. The End.

Dial M For Murder

An introverted woman's husband devises an ingenious plot to kill her. The scheme requires her to answer the phone at a pre-arranged time when the killer will be ready to strike and the husband will have a rock-solid alibi. However the husband realizes his introverted wife will do anything to avoid talking on the phone, so he abandons his perfect murder and resorts instead to divorce. The woman finds she enjoys living alone and develops a fondness for Hermes Kelly bags. The End.

The Constant Gardener

An introverted minor British diplomat in Kenya takes great pleasure in his horticultural hobby. Through a series of flashbacks the mystery of how he started his garden is revealed. Although it soon emerges that a multinational pharmaceutical company did very bad things, he is determined to cultivate the best garden in Kenya, with no thought for the consequences. The End.

Risky Business

Introverted teen's parents leave him alone in the house for the weekend. He is full of hormones. Much internet downloading ensues. He also reads business books and binge-watches Netflix. At the end of the weekend the parents come home and wonder where all the tissues have gone. Young man learns that too much private internet time can be risky. The End.

Dead Poets Society

Young introverted fellow has inspiring but unorthodox new teacher who, it turns out, was once a member of a secret Dead Poets Society. Although the boy is intrigued, he's not into joining groups so does not attempt to restart the club. The teacher imparts wisdom and the boys thrive, content to read their poetry quietly and separately, in their own rooms. No one gets fired and no one dies. No desks are mistreated. The End.

Introvert Horoscope

Welcome to this month's* Introvert Horoscope!

Aries

You will unaccountably feel like staying in and will have to cancel plans at the last moment. No one will be surprised. Seriously, just no one.

Taurus

Someone will say something innocent that you will overanalyze and work yourself up about and cause yourself to feel awful over. Jupiter's continued transit will reveal it all to be nothing.

---

* *Identical to last month's.*

Gemini

Despite your best efforts you will attend a party. You will spend it in the hosts' bedroom where you will happen upon a good selection of books and do some great reading. As you head home you will think, *That wasn't so bad* and wonder why you hate parties so much.

Cancer

The stars** will align and you will get to bed early and sleepily. However as soon as your head hits the pillow it will fill with all the fears and anxieties you've successfully suppressed all day. You will still be awake at 3 am.

Leo

You will go to a shopping mall and become completely overwhelmed by rudeness and noise. People will piss you off. Seriously, what is wrong with people. According to the heavens, that is.

Virgo

You will accidentally let an important call go to voicemail. And by accidentally I mean deliberately.

** *Stars unspecified at time of writing.*

And by an important call I mean all the calls. And by voicemail I mean that thing on your phone that you never check in case it means you have to return a call.

Libra

Your friend will introduce you to a new person. You will hate them preemptively, to save time. You are wise. And efficient. The stars say so.

Scorpio

A new project will require you to work in a group at your job. Using great care and precision, you will gnaw your own arm off to avoid this fate.

Sagittarius

You will feel compelled to do something nerdy and it will give you immense pleasure. Refreshed, you will decide to go out but will quickly feel all peopled out. You will have to immediately return home and binge-watch entire seasons of *Better Call Saul/Game of Thrones/Rake**** to recover.

*** *I don't know which one. Geez, I'm a fake astrologer, not a fake clairvoyant.*

Capricorn

Even though there are many free tables in the cafe, a large noisy group will choose the table right next to you. You will entertain elaborate fantasies of disembowelment and plucking out of eyeballs. The expression on your face will cause you to repeatedly be asked if you are okay.

Aquarius

Despite your earbuds, book, and carefully cultivated resting bitch face, someone will attempt to engage you in friendly chit-chat. They will chat on and on, oblivious to your avoided eye contact, watch-checking, and stifled yawns. Eventually you will pretend to take a phone call and walk away. They probably won't notice.

Pisces

You will read a horoscope that is utter bunkum. You will label it complete poppycock. You will briefly consider that your adjectives are old-fashioned and need updating, but you will dismiss the idea as a load of old hornswoggle.

Confessions Of An Introvert: 11 Not-Very-Nice Things I Have Done

I'm not proud of this, but I've done some not-very-nice things to preserve my introvert sanity.

Okay, maybe I'm a little proud of a couple of them. Or at least, I've made peace with the fact that I was doing my best at the time. A couple are one-off offenses but most are examples of social infractions I've committed many, many times.

Anyway, I'm owning up to these questionable antics in the hope that you can make peace with your own introvert tendencies. Or possibly to trade ideas, I'm not sure yet. Depends what you come up with.

11 Things I've Done to Keep my Introvert Sanity

#1

Ducked into a store to avoid someone I knew on the street because I didn't want to chit-chat. Grabbed something off the rack and fled into a change room when I thought they might be peering in the window to see if it was me. Later returned the iridescent green jumpsuit to the sales assistant, whispering *It's a little snug for me* as I left.

#2

Snuck out of an expensive social event without saying goodbye after only ten minutes because it was too loud and crowded to have a genuine conversation with anyone. Made the taxi driver wait while I picked up KFC on the way home. Consoled myself with a bucket of Hot & Spicy until I felt whole again. Also a little ill.

#3

Felt cranky about having to attend an event I had organized in the first place. Instantly regretted my crazy and short-lived bout of sociability. Resented everyone for backing me into a corner by selfishly and thoughtlessly accepting my invitation.

#4

Accepted an invitation and then canceled plans at the last moment after an extended period of self-searching, self-justification, and general self-loathing.

Repeated the cycle endlessly for years, with complete amnesia every time.

#5

Manifested genuine illnesses of varying virulence and closeness to death in order to have a legitimate excuse for above plan-canceling. Gave small, Norma Desmond-like sighs from my convalescent couch as I recuperated from my bubonic symptoms.

#6

Spent entire dinner parties talking to the hosts' kids. Texted hosts the following day to apologize for several inappropriate things that had been said. By the kids, I mean. Sheesh, kids today!

#7

Stole a bottle of champagne and hung out with fishermen on their boat to escape yet more socializing at a corporate team-building weekend. Sang "Sister Golden Hair" with the fisher dudes. Was asked to stop. Nicely, though. They were polite fisher dudes, and to be fair you probably need your ears to stop bleeding if you want to focus on catching fish.

#8

Pretended not to understand the instructions when told to "find a partner" in a group fitness class. Fostered a confused look when asked to "form a circle". Maintained an expression for the rest of the class that suggested recent and not entirely successful brain surgery so people would keep their distance.

#9

Accidentally elbowed the person next to me at a play when I felt he was in my personal space. Vehemently denied it when my husband, frowning and rubbing his arm in confusion, asked what I did that for.

#10

Faked an elaborate coughing and sneezing fit when someone looked like they were going to sit next to me at a not-very-crowded movie. Glared passive-aggressively at them when they sat there anyway. Was so distracted by my intense protocol of huffing and glaring that I missed most of the movie. Fortunately it was *Glitter* so I totally won that one.

#11

Set up an extended perimeter in an uncrowded Body Pump class so nobody could set up too close to me. Fashioned my boundary from excess weights and sparc bars. Looked nonplussed when the class finished and it turned out I had no use for all that extra equipment.

Come on, admit it — you've done something similar! Haven't you ...?

How To Introvert Like A Boss. And Also Be A Boss

There's a lot of talk these days about how introverts make good leaders, great bosses, yada yada yada. That may be true, but I'm not sure the underlying reasons are the ones most people think.

In an attempt to blow the lid off the truth, I've decoded the subtext for you— the underlying *real, secret reasons* why introverts make excellent bosses. But let's just keep the truth between us.

8 (Secret) Reasons Introverts Make Great Leaders

1. Introverts are always super prepared

Subtext

Introvert leaders tend to prepare thoroughly before they arrive at meetings and conferences.

This is partly because they overthink and overanalyze everything, occasionally chewing off fingernails and losing hair in clumps in the process. But bandaged cuticles and surprising berets aside, boy, are they ready.

2. Introverts host efficient meetings

Subtext

Introvert leaders keep the agenda tight and the momentum flowing.

This is because they *cannot wait* to get the hell out of there. The more efficient the meeting, the quicker they can get back to hiding behind their monitors and working alone in their offices.

3. Introverts listen to their employees

Subtext

Introvert leaders will do anything to get the attention off themselves and onto someone else.

For this reason they are encouraging and attentive when others speak. *Anyone else got something to say? Anyone? Anyone? ANYONE??*

4. Introverts encourage staff to excel

Subtext

Well not just Excel, but any spreadsheet package. In fact any software.

Introvert leaders like to keep staff occupied with the latest programs and challenging projects. This ensures less chattering and keeps the noise level down to a low, comforting hum.

5. Introverts are great at building long-term relationships

Subtext

Introvert leaders are highly adept at dodging small talk and chit-chat.

This means short-term employees may never actually get to speak to them. In fact, it's only after people have been with the company for a while that introvert leaders find something genuine and meaningful to talk to them about. But *quietly*.

6. Introverts get stuff done

Subtext

Introvert leaders are super focused and tend to really power through.

You name it — entire series on Netflix, hefty novels, creative projects, and prodigious amounts of snacks. Their solid training in these areas helps to make introvert leaders highly effective at getting work stuff done, too.

7. Introverts are very thorough

Subtext

Introvert leaders don't take short cuts. This is especially true if it means they might run into others from the office.

They'll happily take the long, winding, savagely overgrown road that's much, much, *much* less travelled. Which makes them extremely diligent and may also explain why they return from lunch with all those scratches.

8. Introverts minimize conflicts

Subtext

If there's drama happening or confrontation brewing, you can count on introvert leaders to be far away.

This lets them avoid the brouhaha and focus instead on strategic thinking, excellent work, and meaningful relationships.

Which is precisely how they become such awesome introvert leaders in the first place.

Newton's 3 Laws Of Motion For Introverts

Isaac Newton's 3 Laws Of Motion transformed our understanding of the world, and also of apples. For the first time we truly understood the hazards of the outdoors, and the very real potential for head injury related to ripe, pendulous fruit.

But have you heard of his less famous 3 Laws of *Introvert* Motion? These are the laws of physics that apply specifically to introverts.

No doubt as you read them you'll recognize their inherent truth, and will nod silently to yourself as you recall with a smile the relevant chapter of *Principia Mathematica*.

Here they are, brilliantly translated for you from the original Latin.

Newton's 3 Laws of Introvert Motion

1. For every introvert action that involves being happy at home …

For every introvert action that involves being happy at home or contentedly pursuing a quiet interest by yourself, there is an *equal and opposite reaction* from someone telling you to push through your comfort zone or come out of your shell.

The expanded comfort zone could include parties, small talk, and even group work, which may or may not occur on an incline.

The introvert may deflect such unwanted advice with a lighthearted quip, or they may prefer to use gravity.

2. The likelihood that someone will take the nearest seat …

The likelihood that someone will take the nearest seat/self-serve checkout/cafe table when there are plenty of free ones farther away is *inversely proportional* to your degree of introversion.

Introverts often attempt to repel these interlopers with annoyed sighs, passive-aggressive mutterings, and dirty looks.

The law of conservation of energy states that such attempts will be met with complete and utter obliviousness.

3. An introvert at rest and enjoying peace and solitude …

An introvert at rest and enjoying peace and solitude will never be allowed to continue at rest but will instead be *acted upon by a force*.

A *kinetic* force may be a loud and vexatious person who wants to chit chat despite the fact you're clearly reading a book and/or have earbuds in.

A *potential* force may be someone knocking at your door despite your being still and staying very very quiet.

Don't Fight Introvert Laws

Once you understand that these are universal introvert laws, you can give up trying to fight against them.

The best you can do is accept this is how things work, and not expect life to be different.

And, as much as possible, stay away from fruit trees.

Source: *Principia Mathematica Introvertica*

How To Survive Group Fitness If You're An Introvert

Many years ago, when I was looking for a way to support my cheese, chocolate and wine habits, I discovered group fitness classes.

In many respects these classes were ideal. They were choreographed to music — I could sing along and forget how hard I was working. They were challenging — there was always something to work on so I stayed motivated. They burned major calories — I could indulge my dietary foibles and still fit into my jeans. In fact, group fitness classes ticked all the "fitness" boxes.

The problem was the *other* part of group fitness: the "group" part. The unfortunate fact that group fitness classes invariably involved, you know, *other people.*

People who tried to talk to you. People who eschewed deodorant or toothpaste or shampoo. People who had no sense of personal space.

People.

But because the classes suited me in so many other ways, I persevered, and over the years I developed strategies for coping with some of the more challenging aspects of group fitness.

Below I've set out some common hazards, with my tried-and-tested solutions for coping with them. Well, some of them. I hope these tips save you some distress.

Introvert Solutions to Common Group Fitness Dilemmas

1. Attempted Conversation

Upon entering a group fitness studio, there is a clear and present danger that a stranger will try to engage you in chit-chat.

They may attempt to share an anecdote about their parking experience, or to conjecture as to whether the air conditioning is working, or, most distressing, to ask you questions, such as how long have you been doing the class or where did you get that top or can they borrow your towel.

Once they have begun speaking, there is little you can do to avoid engagement, unless you're prepared to commit to extreme tactics such as pretending you don't speak English. Better if you can ward off such incursions before they start.

How?

First, avoid eye contact. This of course is simply good practice in all potential social situations, and here it can deter the casual, half-hearted chatster. However, your more determined chit-chatters will proceed even without eye contact.

Which is why you need a second, back-up-strategy: have earbuds in. Earbuds too are a sound pre-emptive strategy for use whenever you may be exposed to sudden stranger interaction.

Combined with eye-contact avoidance, this double defense should insulate you from all but the most hell-bent chit-chat assaults. Keep eyes down and buds in right until the class is about to start.

2. Personal Space Invaders

Perhaps the most insidious source of trouble for the introverted group fitness aficionado is the personal space invader. This is the person who likes to stand near you. *Really* near you.

When you move away to get more space from them, they take it as an invitation to move too. *Oh, we're moving over there now*, they seem to say. Wherever you go, they go, preserving the same minuscule band of distance like a really annoying, sweaty shadow.

Over the years I've had several of these shadows who insisted on standing right near me in every class.

First I tried a passive approach: making a scowling face, huffing melodramatically, complaining loudly to a third party. While I found these tactics stressful, they failed entirely to register on the space invader.

Next, getting more desperate, I worked myself up to an assertive approach: explaining politely that as the class was not crowded I would like more space, and asking if they could please leave a greater distance between us. They smiled and nodded and smiled again and proceeded to make zero adjustment.

Finally I resorted to a slightly aggressive approach: a combination of singing along loudly to the songs in my tuneless, quite horrific singing voice, while also gratuitously swinging my sweaty ponytail in their direction.

Not even that worked.

You may have better luck than I did so my best advice is to keep these strategies in your toolkit: huffing, politely requesting, using sweat as a perimeter marker. Be prepared to experiment, to mix and match.

But I suggest also facing a disturbing reality: some people just like being super close to sweaty strangers. Weird but true.

3. The Dreaded High-Five

As the class progresses, sometimes a group fitness instructor will encourage participants to celebrate their hard work by giving someone a high-five.

Now I understand this is a pleasant and even fun thing for many extroverts to do.

But for the introvert, high-fiving a stranger, like any form of forced interaction, is akin to spraying pepper directly into your own eyes.

The trick to avoiding the high-five is to act fast. Once someone is approaching you, palm raised, smile beaming, you're a goner. You'll have no choice but to assemble your face into a smile, offer your palm, and think of a fort.

Instead, be on high alert for the "high-five" phrase and as soon as you hear it, move swiftly into action. Flee from the center of the class to where you've left your stuff. Then, *facing away* from the class, pick up your towel and wipe off sweat, or grab your water bottle for a big, long drink. (If you face the class you leave yourself open to the travelling high-fiver for whom distance is no object.)

TIP: Be prepared for re-wiping sweat areas or savoring an extra-long drink if the high-fiving is prolonged or multiple high-fives are being encouraged.

4. Forming a Circle

Occasionally a group fitness class will devolve into an orgy of unwanted interaction known as "forming a circle".

When this happens you can no longer remain in your own little world of the music and the mirror's reflection and will be forced to acknowledge the presence of many strangers.

Over the years I've experimented with different strategies for evading the circle. I've developed a cramp and had to stretch. I've needed to check my phone for some sudden and unexplained reason, and been detained there, staring fixedly at the screen, until the circle disbanded.

However, in the end I've found the best solution is to join the circle but at a safe distance, like a little antisocial satellite on the edge of the class orbit. Technically you're part of the group thing, facing in and all. But you can also keep your distance and avoid complete stranger overwhelm.

5. Finding a Partner

For the introvert in a group fitness class, the only words more terrifying than "form a circle" are "find a partner".

Fortunately though, there's a quick, effective strategy for subverting this command: simply look confused and avoid eye contact for the time it takes people to partner up.

If everyone gets partnered up then you're golden; you can relax and stop looking confused and resume your workout solo.

If there's one person left over and looking lost, then resolutely maintain your eye-contact-avoiding confusion just a little longer. Eventually the instructor will partner with the residual person and you'll be left blessedly partner-free.

Leaving you alone to finish the class in your lovely, happy, pretend-it's-not-a-group, group-fitness bubble.

18 Amazing Inventions For Introverts I Am Currently Working On

1. Insomnia Cut-and-Paste Tool

Cuts time from when you're flagrantly insomniac in the middle of the night and pastes it onto that deeply comatose moment just before the alarm is about to go off.

2. Party Survival Pod

Compact, lightweight, self-assembling introvert survival kit that includes books, quality snacks, beverages, noise-canceling headphones, and fold-out comfy armchair. Fits unobtrusively into any party corner.

3. Personal Space Protection Bubble

Lightly stabs anyone entering your personal space without prior approval.

4. Flashing Fluro High-Pitched Earbud Arrow

Appears above your head, flashes in neon colors, and emits a loud, high-pitched squeal when people don't notice your earbuds and attempt to talk at you regardless.

5. i(ntrovert)Phone

Comes with phone app irretrievably disabled so you can never ever never receive a telephone call.

6. Go-Dark Switch

Instantly mutes all TV/stereo/devices, turns out all lights, and closes all blinds and curtains when an unexpected visitor knocks.

7. Cinema Seat Allocator

Sequentially deactivates seat spikes in order to ensure maximum space between theatre patrons. Can be adapted for cafes, trains, buses, lecture halls, etc.

8. Quippy Comeback Time-Space Expander

Creates a temporary rip in the time-space continuum until you inevitably think of an awesome comeback later that day in the shower, so you can make a clever retort in what looks like real time.

9. Invisibilizer

Activates a cloaking device that makes you instantly vanish when someone tries to engage you in chit-chat.

10. Internet Shallowness Filter

Removes from the visible spectrum all depth-sucking distractions, including teen celebrities thrilled to have "finally" made it, celebrities with perfect marriages, celebrities with formerly perfect marriages who are now divorcing, and celebrities who have gained or lost weight or released a new handbag collection.

11. Judgmental Inner Voice Silencer

Actually someone beat me to this invention. Also known as wine.

12. De-Overthinkifier

Recognizes when you are overthinking, overanalyzing, unconstructively ruminating, or working yourself up over nothing (i.e. when you are awake) and reassigns all active brain cells to watching a randomly generated episode of *The Simpsons*.

13. Sidewalk Navigator Javelin

Allows you to forge a path through clueless pedestrians, slow-walkers, escalator spreaders, and sidewalk blockers.

14. Unwanted Advice Deflector

Causes an intense personal itch in anyone who tells you to come out of your shell or otherwise instructs you on how to live your life.

15. Fake Exuberance Teleporter

Instantly teleports you to safety whenever you are expected to whoop, high-five, applaud something you don't want to applaud, do the macarena, or throw your hands in the air like you just don't care.

16. Snack Inventorizer

Automatically monitors snack levels and prompts you to re-stock whenever supplies of your favorite snacks fall below a certain crucial level.

17. Sales Assistant Deactivator

Painlessly neutralizes store sales assistants so they're unable to ask if you're having an awesome day, or if you need help within 4.7 seconds of entering a change room, or to follow you around the store, or to list in elaborate detail the benefits of an item you've already discarded.

18. Self-Writing Doctor's Note

Exempts you from all forms of small-group activities, ice-breakers, trust exercises, or anything requiring you to "find a partner".

*

Enquiries from venture capitalists welcome.

All patents pending.

37 Introvert Proverbs: Wisdom For The Socially Disinclined

Here are 37 pieces of wisdom for introverts and other socially disinclined individuals ...

1. A wink is as good as a nod to a blind man but both can be dodged by studiously avoiding eye contact.
2. Patience is a virtue as well as one of many games you can play entirely on your own.
3. A drowning man will clutch at a straw so avoid the ocean and always keep your cocktail close.
4. Charity begins at home so be virtuous and just stay in.
5. You can't judge a book by its cover but you can use it to try and escape other people's attempts at conversation on planes.
6. A bird in the hand means the outdoors is not for you and you should probably not be allowed near the fauna again.
7. Don't bite the hand that feeds you but it's okay to lick the cheese off it when you're having pizza.

8. Don't put the cart before the horse unless it's your Amazon cart and you're stocking up on books. I don't know how the horse got involved here.

9. Don't cross the bridge until you come to it. Or stay home and don't cross the bridge at all, which also avoids bridge trolls with their weird troll hair.

10. Empty vessels make the most sound so enjoy greater quiet by always keeping your wineglass filled.

11. A friend in need is a friend indeed but it's definitely best if they text rather than call.

12. Absence makes the heart grow fonder. This one seems good as is.

13. One cannot live on bread alone, but wine, cheese and chocolate will do the trick.

14. Do unto others as you would have them do to you: never drop in unannounced and always text rather than call.

15. Good things come to those who wait so best to cancel your plans and stay home and wait for the postman.

16. Blood is thicker than water but wine tastes so much better than both.

17. As one door closes another opens so lock them all and be very, very quiet until the knocking stops.

18. Home is where the heart is. Also the wi-fi, Netflix, books, and good snacks.

19. Hope for the best and prepare for the worst by always ordering extra pizza.
20. It never rains but it pours, which is a lovely time to read a book and sip coffee or tea by the window.
21. Early to bed, ~~early to rise, makes you healthy, wealthy and wise,~~ but then read till 3 am.
22. Give a man a fish and he will eat for a day and therefore leave you alone so you can binge-watch your stories.
23. Fall seven times, get up eight, and then that's enough wine for you.
24. Half a loaf is better than none but why not just order pizza instead.
25. The "proof" of the alcohol is in the drinking.
26. To add insult to injury, try a kick in the shins followed by yelling, *Ew, you smell*. It's one way to get people to leave you alone.
27. An apple a day keeps the doctor away and staying very quiet when strangers knock also helps.
28. Too many cooks spoil the broth because the broth just wants to be left alone.
29. The early bird catches the worm so sleep in and by the time you're up all the worms will be gone.
30. You can't have your cake and eat it too so for the love of Pete just buy extra cake.
31. It takes two to tango but only one to stay home, eat snacks, and binge-watch Netflix.

32. The pen is mightier than the sword, which is why pretty stationery is fierce.

33. There's no use crying over spilt milk but spill a good Shiraz and it's perfectly fine to bawl your eyes out.

34. Two heads are better than one because that's twice as many coins for tipping the pizza dude.

35. If at first you don't succeed try re-booting the wi-fi router.

36. Never put off till tomorrow what you can binge-watch today.

37. You made your bed now you must lie in it, so take a good book and enjoy!

The Introvert's Guide To Networking Events

Here are the steps. Follow them carefully!

1. Open invitation to networking event.
2. Carefully read all event information so there are no surprises.
3. Check diary for other commitments to properly manage energy.
4. Visualize yourself making small talk at networking event.
5. Become aghast at the prospect, decide not to go.
6. Toss invitation.
7. Relax and read a book to recover from the ordeal.

7 Ingenious Introvert Apps Someone Needs To Create

Can you imagine how much better life would be for introverts if the awesome apps described below were available? Here's how I imagine these apps would work ...

1. The Virtual Boundary App

What it is

This app is like those virtual fences that give the family pet a mild zap when it reaches the yard's virtual boundary.

But where electronic fences protect pets from life-threatening hazards beyond the lawn, the Virtual Boundary app protects introverts from soul-threatening hazards of people without personal space awareness.

How it works

The app registers when someone enters your personal zone, locks on the identified interloper, and administers a mild shock. Nothing too bad, just the electrical equivalent of *uh-uh buddy, that's too close.*

There are settings for public transport, movie theatre, shopping mall, sidewalk, etc.

The app also recognizes your "favorites" from your contact list and excludes them from the shocks.

Or does it?

Better check your settings.

2. The Small Talk Deflector App

What it is

This app helps secure the introvert against the dreaded scourge of pointless chit-chat.

How it works

The app requires enabling the microphone, remains on in the background, and works by voice recognition.

It's triggered by phrases involving the weather, questions about where you live or what you do for a living, and other generic nuggets of small talk.

Once triggered, the app emits a high-pitched shriek so that conversation cannot continue. This allows the introvert to take out their phone, make a puzzled face at the sound, and wander away bewildered — and entirely without explanation.

3. The All-Peopled-Out Safe Word App

What it is

This app generates a faux emergency so an introvert who has reached *maximum people level* can quickly and safely escape.

How it works

In the same way that Siri can be turned on by the iPhone owner's voice, this app can be triggered by the introvert's voice saying a pre-set "safe" word.

Good safe-word choices include *solitude, recluse,* and *misanthrope.*

Any time you find yourself peopled out, simply say your safe word and the app randomly generates a benign and true-ish emergency text.

Faux emergencies include:

- A text from "The Office" saying you need to come in immediately to fix a *glitch-related snafu* (this is true because who hasn't had their share of glitch-related snafus?)

- A text from "Security" saying some *unusual activity* has been detected on your wi-fi (this of course is true because it's unusual that you're not at home using the wi-fi)
- A text from "Doctor" saying your *test results* are in and they're not good (this is also true because the test results are indeed not good, they're great, as only completely made-up test results can be).

Because the emergencies are randomly generated, the introvert can react with genuine surprise as they brandish their emergency text and beat their hasty retreat.

4. The Party Avoidance Calendar App

What it is

This app allows the introvert to dodge Tupperware parties, baby showers, rambunctious nights out, and other group activities requiring you to close your book, put on pants, and be with people.

How it works

It is essentially a faux calendar app that has every time slot filled with work, exercise, social events, medical appointments, coffee dates, weekends away, skydiving courses, *The Voice* auditions, and sundry other engagements.

If invited in person you can simply open the app and point disappointingly at the relevant previous engagement as you shake your head sadly.

If e-vited, do not fret — see the next app idea.

5. The Party Avoidance e-Vite Autoresponder App

What it is

This app facilitates the dodging of invitations received by email. It works in sync with the introvert's email client, adding an Avoid Party button to the Reply/Forward options.

How it works

Upon receiving an invitation, you simply click the Avoid Party button. This generates one of those "Unable to deliver message" messages, with a whole lot of technical-looking gobbledygook relating to full mailboxes or proxy servers or whatever.

Easy. Efficient. Evasive.

6. The 5 Stages of Canceling Plans App

What it is

This app helps the introvert navigate the difficult but necessary stages they must work through once they inadvertently commit themselves to plans.

How it works

Any time that plans are entered into the introvert's calendar, the app is triggered and generates a sequence of stages for the introvert:

Stage 1: Commitment

Stage 2: Seeking Reassurance

Stage 3: Mild Panic

Stage 4: Blind Terror and Frantic Attempts At Escape

Stage 5: Cancellation and Relief.

The introvert is prompted by pop-up reminders to check off their progress as they make their way through each of the stages.

By allowing the introvert to acknowledge their passage through these stages, the app helps the introvert to manage their psychological distress and once again find a sense of wholeness.

7. The Clueless-Walkers Bicycle Bell App

What it is

This ingenious app helps the introvert to maneuver their way through sidewalks, shopping centers, in fact anywhere people wander aimlessly or inconsiderately and impede passage.

How it works

The app is activated by double-tapping the play button on the remote, which produces a sharp bicycle bell sound. This breaks the loiterer out of their reverie and causes them to register the surprising presence of other people who also wish to use the sidewalk/escalator/pathway.

*

Introverts are an untapped market in the app space. Take note savvy developers!

Introvert Dictionary: 21 Key Terms Every Introvert Should Know

How good is your introvert vocabulary? Have you mastered the language of introvert-speak?

Check your knowledge with these 21 important terms from the introvert lexicon — terms that every introvert should know ...

1. Plans

Engagements for dates in a vague, hypothetical future that Future You commits to but Present You hopes will never come.

2. Canceling

What you have to do when it turns out the future is imminent and Present You lacks the psychological resources to see through the plans that Future You made.

3. Party

Social event that is too loud, with too many people, and too little opportunity for genuine conversation.

4. Friends

Very small number of people with whom you like to spend quality time talking about things that matter.

5. Doorbell

Sound to strike terror into the heart unless you are expecting someone. Preferably someone who's delivering a package of books or bringing pizza. Ideally both.

6. TV Show

Wondrous world where you can be with people without having to be with actual people.

7. Book

Wondrous world where you can be inside someone *else's* head. Especially pleasurable when it's raining outside. Sometimes made into a film by someone who optioned it because it was a bestseller but didn't actually get what made it a great book.

8. Home

Awesome place of wi-fi and books and TV shows and snacks.

9. Fantastrophize

Launch into elaborate daydream in which horrific events unfold, out of all proportion to probability and unsupported by immediate facts.

10. Solitude

Introvert battery charger. Works for all introvert models.

11. Extrovert

Person who is comfortable with a much higher level of stimulation than an introvert, whether from noise, lights, people, plans, tasks, or other sources.

12. Shell

The extremely pleasurable thing people keep telling you to come out of.

13. Overthinking

Loop of mental processing, re-processing, double-processing, back-processing, and re-processing again, often about something minor, and frequently continued until you have worked yourself into a state of complete distress.

14. Phone

Together with the Stocks app, the least-used app on your phone.

15. Voicemail Message

Recorded outgoing request that people text you instead.

16. Strangers

People who stand waaaaay too close.

17. Earbuds

Magical devices that communicate: *Please don't speak to me.* Occasionally the magic malfunctions and said earbuds become invisible to certain people, who then attempt to speak to you, usually loudly so you can hear them over the earbuds they supposedly can't see, and often without saying *excuse me*.

18. Group Projects

Circle 4 in The Introvert's 9 Circles of Hell, where introvert souls are condemned to complete tasks with other people, despite being willing to do all the work themselves in exchange for being allowed to work alone.

19. Nerd

Term used by some people to denigrate introverts, but taken as a compliment by introverts who celebrate their own interests, hobbies, and creativity.

20. Small Talk

Topics of conversation in which neither party has genuine interest. Can cause the introvert's pores to secrete portions of their soul.

21. Happiness

The contentment found in different places for different people. Which for the introvert is usually at home, surrounded by books and the remote and plenty of excellent snacks.

The Adventures Of Kurt The Introverted Donkey: Kurt And The Bullies

There once was an introverted little donkey named Kurt.

When Kurt was just a little foal he used to go to mule school. He wasn't into team sports and preferred to read during recess.

His favorite books were *Goodnight Mule*, *Donkey and the Chocolate Factory*, *The Velveteen Donkey*, and especially *The Wind in the Burros*, which was about some donkeys who ate a lot of baked beans.

After school, when many of the other little donkeys hung out at the mule mall, Kurt liked to go home and watch TV with a nice snack of mixed hay and straw. Or to hang out with his pals, Herb and Lamont.

Kurt's behavior bothered some of the other donkeys. They would chant taunts as Kurt tried to read his book:

Kurt, Kurt, the introvert! Kurt, Kurt, the introvert!

They would steal his lunch money to spend on arcade games like Donkey Kong, and yell as they ran off:

Kurt, Kurt, the introvert! Kurt, Kurt, the introvert!

They would follow him home, pretty much out of bullying ideas — for they were not intellectually gifted donkeys, as bullies seldom are. They'd call at him softly, so grown-up donkey neighbors couldn't hear — for they were cowardly donkeys, as bullies often are:

whispered surreptitiously
Kurt, Kurt, the introvert! Kurt, Kurt, the introvert!

One afternoon Kurt and Lamont were doing online research for a paper on donkey suffrage and the rise of the donkey vote.

"Why the long face?" asked Lamont. He was not being ironic, for Lamont was blessed with neither wit nor looks. But he was rich in kindness and could be surprisingly insightful.

"Oh, no reason really," said Kurt. He didn't look away from the screen. "It's just … those donkey bullies call me names."

"What names?" asked Lamont. He wondered if Lamont was one of the names. If so, he didn't see the problem.

"They call me 'Kurt, Kurt, the introvert'."

"What does that mean?" As his own name was no longer a possibility, Lamont had pretty much lost interest in the conversation. But he sensed it was important to his sad friend.

"Well, you know, it's someone who likes to be on their own. Not really a joiner. And maybe they like nerdy things."

"What's wrong with that?" Lamont had crossed his legs and put on Kurt's glasses. He was trying to look like an empathetic donkey therapist.

Kurt looked away from the screen at his friend. He couldn't help but smile.

But it was a good question. What *was* wrong with being an introvert?

It meant he enjoyed his own company, was independent, resourceful. It meant he had few friends but he was a *good* friend. It meant he was never really bored.

Kurt gave a delighted bray.

"Lamont, you're a genius!" said Kurt.

Lamont blushed and turned back to the screen, which he was completely unable to read due to Kurt's prescription glasses. However, he didn't want to move an inch. He wanted only to bask in his friend's compliment, which he felt no pressure to analyze or question in any way.

The next day Kurt was reading his book as usual when the donkey bullies appeared and began their taunts.

Kurt, Kurt, the introvert! Kurt, Kurt, the introvert!

Kurt looked up from his book and into the eyes of his harassers. His little donkey voice quivered.

"Yes, I am an introvert. I don't enjoy big groups or a lot of noise. I like simple things. I have a few friends, but they're the best friends a donkey could want. I know how to be happy on my own. In fact, I love being an introvert!"

The bullies glared at Kurt in stunned silence. A bully victim speaking up like this was unprecedented. A large tumbleweed blew past, which one of the bullies grabbed and ate (it was full of hay). No one moved for what seemed like donkey's years.

"You … know how to be happy on your own?" asked Stanley, the head bully. His thick donkey eyebrow was raised.

"Um. Sure," said Kurt. "I have heaps of interests. I mean they might not be things you'd like, but they make me happy."

"Huh," said Stanley. "If I knew how to be happy on my own I wouldn't waste so much time with these losers. I mean, they really are asses."

The other donkeys shifted uncomfortably.

Kurt closed his book and held it out. "You can try reading this if you like."

Stanley took the book, *Donkey Copperfield*, holding it with great care. His nostrils flared. "Reading … *me*?"

Kurt smiled uncertainly. He wasn't sure how to wrap up a foiled bully session. He waited.

"Well, I guess I'm gonna go find Lamont," said Kurt finally. "I promised to help him with his science project."

The bully donkeys moved to the side so Kurt could pass. He trotted along for a little while, then turned back to look at the bully donkeys. They were all braying at Stanley, who was just standing there quietly, looking down at the book in his hooves.

*

For the next few days a few of the bully donkeys continued to yell half-hearted insults at Kurt.

Kurt, Kurt, likes frozen yogurt.
Kurt, Kurt, he wears a shirt.

But they knew the invectives were lame and soon they gave up and joined a tail-chasing league.

And what of Stanley?

He was never seen with the bullies again. He was too busy in the library, helping to re-shelve books and slowly reading his way through the donkey decimal system.

List of References

How To Understand The Psychology Of Introverts

For more on personality:

Carver, C. S. and Schier, M.F. (2004). Perspectives on Personality (5th ed). US: Pearson.

Cervone, D. and Pervin, L.A. (2013). Personality Theory and Research (12th ed). US: Wiley.

Haslam, N. (2007). Introduction to Personality and Intelligence. UK: Sage.

How To Switch Off And Sleep Better

Thanks to Cal Newport for the idea of the "shut-down ritual":
Newport, C., 2016. *Deep Work*. 1st ed. GB: Little, Brown.

The Introvert's 9 Circles Of Hell

Thanks to this site for the descriptions of Dante's circles:
Dante's Inferno. *The Levels of Hell*. [ONLINE] Available at: http://www.danteinferno.info/circles-of-hell/. [Accessed 30 July 2018].

18 Amazing Inventions For Introverts I Am Currently Working On

Thanks to Jack Handey for the inspiration:

Jack Handey. 2016. *Inventions of Mine That Have Been Misused for Evil Purposes*. [ONLINE] Available at: https://www.newyorker.com/magazine/2016/05/30/my-inventions-misused-for-evil-by-jack-handey. [Accessed 30 July 2018].

Michele Connolly is the founder of popular websites LouderMinds.com for introverts and GetOrganized-Wizard.com for decluttering and getting organized. She has a Bachelor of Psychology and has written a thesis on personality and happiness. She is an introvert, minimalist, overthinker, sharer of micro-epiphanies, and embracer of personal weirdness. You can find her at MicheleConnolly.com.

Printed in Great Britain
by Amazon